D1336769

The Penny World

Also by Arthur Barton

TWO LAMPS IN OUR STREET

(New Authors)

ARTHUR BARTON

The Penny World

A BOYHOOD RECALLED

'Where is the penny world I bought . . . ?'

T. S. ELIOT

HUTCHINSON OF LONDON

HUTCHINSON & CO (*Publishers*) LTD
178–202 Great Portland Street, London W1

London Melbourne Sydney
Auckland Bombay Toronto
Johannesburg New York

First published 1969

This book has been set in Pilgrim, printed in Great Britain on Antique Wove paper by Anchor Press, and bound by Wm. Brendon, both of Tiptree, Essex

09 097080 2

For Dorothy

Contents

Introduction

Two years ago I wrote my first book, an autobiograpy of my childhood and adolescence in a small mid-Tyne town during the twenties and early thirties. It was loosely chronological and episodic and ended, after the death of my long-widowed mother and several years on the dole, with my taking the motor coach for London and a possible new life.

The book had a modest success—such books are unlikely to become best sellers—but many people seemed to like it, and quite a number wrote to me and said so. Some of these were exiled Geordies of my own generation, some middle-aged people of similar backgrounds from other areas. Few were young, though being young is what the book is all about, and only one was a 'character' from the book itself. This I attribute in part to the fact that there is still no bookshop in the town, though I gather that there is a public library. In my day there were only two small private libraries, one in the Mechanics' Institute (I remember every book being covered in tough homely brown paper) and one in a part of the Co-op Hall where we signed for our dole twice a week. I did a good deal of enjoyable if mainly middle-brow reading in both during my years of idleness.

I could not have survived without books. These, together with what there was of 'nature', for which I had then an almost Wordsworthian passion, friendship, and above all frequent episodes of romantic love, constituted my lifeline. I wrote poems and stories both then and later but being without much initiative or great talent, and, receiving little notice or encouragement, had not the confidence to attempt a book until several B.B.C. producers for whom I had written reminiscences as interval talks, and a representative of my publishers who had heard one or two of them, suggested that it might be done. The result was *Two Lamps in Our Street*, which to my astonishment and delight was very kindly reviewed in the sort of newspapers and literary journals I had read with such awe and jejeune longing as a consciously poetic (and unconsciously rather absurd) youth in the twenties.

It was nice to see my book in shop windows, and though I never saw anyone actually buying it, to know that they were doing so, but all too soon it disappeared from view or was relegated to an anonymous row, from which I was not above abstracting a copy to set up alongside later successes by 'real' writers.

I came to see that I might write another book. Indeed, all the people who wrote to me asked if I would. Some wanted more reminiscences of my young days, others a continuation of the first book. 'What happened to you when you got to London?' was an inevitable question, especially from the young people I teach or have taught in the Cheshire market town where I live now, and one chapter at any rate in this my second book will tell them a little about that: but not much, for my publishers have decided that there is perhaps room for one more book of reminiscences before (if I'm asked) I go on with a later period of my life.

The poem I have included is one I wrote a year or two ago after a visit to Jarrow. On that occasion I wandered about in the much changed town for a few hours, but met no one I ever knew in the past. Inevitably I walked down Grenville Street, now twice its length and with far more than 'two lamps'. The front door of No. 33 is the same one because the deep scratches made by Sweep, my father's black spaniel, are still there. I remembered times when I had clung crying over some forgotten mishap to its black door-knob some little distance above them half a century ago. If I had not hurried away I might have done it again.

Jarrow Revisited

THIS is the best way to come; from the sullen seaside,
Past the wide Slake where black tide-lifted timber
Dries in a wind that still sweeps over the salt-grass
And moans in the lepers' window under the tower.
Here is the handful of stones, the Saxon doorway,
The sketch of a wall and cloister against the sky,
Mackerel over the masts of a Blue Star fruit boat
On the Northumberland side that goes on to the Cheviot,
Where a shepherd may leap the Tyne dry-shod on the
heather.
Here is no change since Bede, the boy from Monkwear-
mouth,
Answered his master's Mass when a plague had killed off
the Chapter,
Lived to be scholar and saint and light of the northland.
Here the Don shines and stinks, that ran clear and
sparkling
Under the Viking keels, where bearded, wing-hatted,
Waited the warriors to burn village and monastery down.
But where are the little white houses where old women,
mostly Irish,
Sat in the sun of a Sunday evening, and nodded
To Protestants off to their candle-less Methodist mission?

And where are the noisy horse-smelling streets of my childhood,
From railway to river close-packed as North Shields' herrings,
Where every man had a place in the great hierarchy
That began at the shipyard gate and ended under the gantries,
While out on the tide swung ships that Jarrow workmen
Fashioned from sweat and steel till the bitter thirties?
Those streets are all gone, and the smoke, and the men for the most part
Sleep on the hill hard by their beloved allotments.
(God give them eternal shine of a Sunday morning,
And the biggest leek in the show, and a winning pigeon,
And a red carnation to set off their Sunday blue,)
Knowing nothing of this new town that I'm almost lost in,
Grown up round two sculptured Vikings and a bowling alley,
That has forgotten Bede, and would like to forget the Marchers.
They've left the churches I see—Christ Church, and St. Peter's,
St. Mark's, and St. John's, and St. Bede's black and Catholic as ever,
Where we fought with bombaters to vindicate George over Patrick.
I'm glad they're still there; I've nothing against the churches,
At least they were open and warm, and sometimes we knew
Exaltation in singing about the Man of Sorrows.
Once, in the Good Shepherd chapel, early, before communion,

When I opened the door I felt that God had just gone;
And we often saw his son in the front of the dole queue
Shuffling upstairs to the money changers,
A suffering silent man, who bowed his head
Meekly before the fat little Jacks-in-office;
Sold for much less than thirty pieces of silver
While Pilate washed his hands in the Ritz hotel:
No, as I've said, I've little against the churches—
In spite of snob vicars, and arrogant visiting bishops,
Preaching about some Codex we'd bought from the
  Russians,
Instead of feeding the sheep, who, like their master
Were homeless, hungry, cold, forsaken, betrayed;
But I've been closer to Christ in shoeless misery
Before the years wove their cocoon of comparative
  comfort
Than I can get now. A door has closed somewhere.
The Vikings I don't much care for. Why isn't it Bede?
We were a brief glory in Europe because of him;
Or couldn't you put up a saint by a bowling alley?
Well then, there are others; what about that philanthropist
  Jarvis,
Great hearted Surrey stranger, who one day adopted
Forty thousand poor Geordies and did what little he could?
Or Godfrey Winn, who gave out the toys one Christmas
At a junior school in one of our decent suburbs?
And didn't Jack Priestley once stand at the top of Ellison
  Street
Making notes for one more warm-hearted article,
While barefoot boys were running like spilled quicksilver
Crying *North Mail* to every point of the compass?
Once, even he came—our Prince, long-coated and hatless,

Walking amongst us ahead of the shipyard gentry;
Looking like death. (Was it hangover or compassion?)
He smiled with Jacobite charm, dear latter-day Charlie;
We hoped, would have followed, but he too never came
  back;
And they closed the yards and left us all at the lane-ends
Doubled up on our hunkers to keep the hunger pains
  down.
Well, the Vikings at least had courage, it might have been
  worse.
I like the new streets, the sanitary flats and houses,
The spaces where suffering has escaped like steam.
I've no time or tears to spare for slums that were land-
  marks,
For Ferry Street, Curry Street, Tyne Street, but I wonder
  where
The old woman's gone who lived through that entry near
  Lipton's
And prayed at her window all night for the people of
  Jarrow?
(In their roystering days that was, when the Rolling Mill
  Tavern
Spilled drunks into Western Road like fish from a trawler.)
There's one cobbled stretch left like an exposed Roman
  pavement
Where I walked with a girl that first and remembered
  time,
And kissed at a corner where now only thin airs meet.
I wonder where she is now, and if ever she wonders
Where I am? because all the hurrying people
I met were strangers. There wasn't a single face looking
  out of my past,

And the young, so touchingly like them,
Never knew hunger or cold or unemployment.
Never went barefoot to school, or watched their mothers
Starving to feed them right through a hopeless winter
When east winds filled the gutters with ice, and small
  children
Sprawled in their shifts and wondered why all this glass
  stuff
Stopped their contented digging with cup and spoon.
This is a new town, and only the old like me
Have a legend the years wrote deep with ten cruel fingers
Like 'Calais' on Mary's heart: and the years again have
  eroded
Some of those words, and soft living covered them over.
Good luck to you, Jarrow. I saw it once written in fireworks;
Before your betrayal that was, when hopeful and young
I ran up the Bede Burn to school on September mornings,
Nor suspected among my subjects were sickness and
  sorrow.
Good luck once again, and remember old Bede our scholar
Who once put us first on the cultural map of Europe,
And Charlie Mark Palmer who made and marred us much
  later.
Remember the valiant shipbuilders who have no head-
  stones
Where rank cemetery grass is stirred, sea-winded;
Remember the streets, the starvation, the wasting disease;
(That Herod who slaughtered our innocents) and think of
  the woman
Who looked from her tenement windows and prayed for
  salvation
For all in your riverside borders, my world, my mother.

Christmas Eve and Christmas Day

THE Christmas Eve I remember best, though it is probably a composite of several similar occasions, is one in 1924 or 1925 when I was a schoolboy; the Christmas Day nearly a decade later when our town was in the depths of its economic depression and behind many a door the crusade to London that was to make this small Tyneside area famous for the third time in its long history was taking shape in the minds of resolute and desperate men. The link between them is that both events began from precisely the same spot.

We always met at midnight to begin our carol singing in the little paved square at the front of Merrick's shop, and even on the coldest night there was a faintly warm smell of new bread coming up from the cooling ovens below. Not for us the genteel singing of carols during the early evening before the last shops had extinguished their gas mantles, and dilatory parents were still buying holly sprays and belated presents, and we greeted certain church choirs on their way home to bed with great condescension.

Twelve o'clock had struck from South Shields town hall clock, coming faintly over the thousands of empty streets and frosty roofs, and the shut shipyards given over to gloom and silence—except where a watchman's fire gleamed or a steel plate boomed like a bell, when we set out. We carried hymn books, lanterns on poles, and an ancient folding harmonium that looked, when borne by four young men, like a small coffin, and gave a mordant and incongruous touch to our muffled cheerful company.

There were about thirty of us, mostly members of Lady Street Methodist mission, and we ranged from old Mr. Bell who remembered that ugly blackened little building when it was new, down to us schoolboys and girls, for whom to stay up all night was in those stricter times very heaven.

We walked in loose couples, led by Mr. Moffat, whose resonant tenor proclaimed itself in his speech and laughter, and Mr. Waterfield always brought up the rear.

He was as old as Mr. Bell but without any of that gentleman's geniality. A lifelong bachelor (it was rumoured that he had been crossed in love back in the eighties) courting couples who tried to linger in inviting porches or doorways got short shrift from him, Yuletide or no.

Nevertheless, carol-singing was a famous time for match-making, and many a hymn book shared under the alternate shadow and shine of inexpertly held lanterns was the modest beginning of lifelong attachments. It took second place only in that respect to the annual pleasure steamer outing up the Tyne to Ryton or Corbridge where most troths were plighted in the buttercup golden fields near the Wall, once the scene of bloody conflict between Pict and Roman.

Like Hardy's Mellstock choir, though very different with our rapid Northumbrian speech and our background of cranes and chimneys, we crept up silently on our victims. With much suppressed laughter and exaggerated pantomime we fanned out round our wheezing instrument, and promptly on the downbeat of Mr. Moffat's tuning fork burst into 'Praise ye the Lord 'tis good to raise'. The tune was 'Good News' with its fine bass run that gave some of the men a chance to show their paces. Christmas had begun.

Through the night we worked our way across town and into the suburbs where foremen, clerks, doctors and such-like aristocracy of our community lived, where the grammar school I went to raised its decent Edwardian tower to the night sky, and even beyond this, to the edge of the few miles of grimy country between our town and the next. Houses were being built here, new, red, and raw as a tanker ready for launching, but it was whispered that they contained bathrooms and rumoured (erroneously) that certain of these were used as supplementary coal cellars.

Beyond them, if the weather was seasonable, one could see shining fields under Orion's glitter and a dim light in some distant inn or farmhouse. For a little while everyone would be quiet, thinking (though, of course, no one would mention it) of Bethlehem and the shepherds.

Standing in the dark on the windy edge of the estate we would hear, faint and far, a rival choir back in town and speculate on its identity. Ears would be cocked, Mr. Waterfield would click open his silver watch and hold it near a lantern, following this action by a complacent nod of the head and the pronouncement,

'Them's the "Uniteds" at Charlie Metcalfe's in Leopold Street. I can pick out Ethel Stewart from here!' This lady was a Wagnerian soprano, the pride and joy of the United Methodist chapel, a wealthy suburban congregation that looked down on our little Wesleyan mission, and boasted about its collections.

Lady Street mission was almost in the shipyards and most of the people who went to it were of the humbler sort, labourers rather than tradesmen, leavened by an occasional shopkeeper or clerk. We could sing, however, and usually contrived to cross our rivals' path during the night, or found them singing at a house near to the one we were making for. If they were already singing, etiquette demanded that we should wait, listen, and make appropriate if not completely sincere murmurs of approbation. This done, with what immediate and un-Christian fervour we would burst into 'Hark the Herald' or 'How beautiful upon the mountains' to show that for all our lowly habitation we were not to be despised as a choir.

Several times during the night we were refreshed, if not with cakes and ale, with the Methodist equivalent—mince pies and ginger wine. I remember, however, that even that innocuous throat-burning concoction was suspect to some. These were still the days of Rechabites whose only drink was 'water bright from the crystal spring'.

I remember how solid and grand the furniture of some foreman's or shopkeeper's parlour would seem to me, how the smells of polish, real carpet (instead of clippy mats), plum cake, oranges and newly washed aspidistras all mingled in a general atmosphere of comfort and ease. There would be a row of devotional books too, the Bible, of course, John Wesley's Journal, Bunyan, and *In Tune with the Infinite*. Some of these men were local preachers —laymen who took our services while the real minister confined himself to the more salubrious St. John's, and how Mr. Micah Robinson (now jovially handing round the mince pies) was powerful in prayer, and Mr. Seth Sparkes, now pouring second glasses of sarsaparilla for us boys, could hold the chapel spellbound with his dramatic reconstruction of the drowning of Egypt's chariots and horses in the Red Sea.

The collecting box would be nearly full of the traditional half-crowns that provided the aged poor of our district with their Boxing Day tea, when we reached Mr. Jamieson's house. He was a big bearded man, who looked like St. Peter or one of the Vikings who had twice burned our town down ages ago in the eighth century. All the week he wore a leather jerkin and delivered coal, but on Sunday he appeared in a suit of deepest black, brilliant boots, and with a huge bible under his arm. His ejaculatory prayers, loud exclamations of 'Glory' or 'Selah', made small children cry. He had a fanatical devotion to the third person of the Trinity, and nervous young ministers had been known to run from chapel pursued by Mr. Jamieson, expository finger raised above the Book open at chapter and verse, convicted of some unconscious heresy. He stood now under the hall light, while we clustered round his front porch, wearing what seemed (but it surely couldn't have been?) a velvet smoking-jacket, and countering Mr. Moffat's offer of any *special* carol with: 'They're aal special ro me, Jack,' which somehow put us in the wrong for preferring some carols to others.

Towards four o'clock a silence would fall on us when we weren't actually singing. The dawn wind was always chilly even on the mildest of Christmases, and frequently bitter. We huddled round the harmonium as if it could give us warmth, and our breaths ascended like sacrificial smoke. Coins were dropped from windows now, and no welcoming doors opened. At last we came full circle back to our chapel again. There it stood, wire-protected windows, faintly Gothic doorway, worn stone steps up which some of our band had struggled in infancy. Round it, protecting rather than menacing, were row on row of small terraced houses leading inevitably down to the river. Up in the sky, among its real luminaries, a gantry-crane light flickered like the star of Bethlehem in a schoolroom play.

Only a mile or two away along the quays John Wesley had preached, and brother Charles, watching the foundry flames shoot up (as they would again in two days' time), had written one of his best-loved hymns.

> 'See how great a flame aspires,
> Kindled by a spark of Grace.'

Sitting in the choir vestry, which exhaled the unusual but delightful odour of hot sausage rolls and brewing tea, we rested from our labours. Mr. Moffat said, as he always did, 'Ye sang well, hinneys,' then fell asleep over his second pint pot, lovers whispered, and schoolboys munched eagerly, anxious to get home to their bulging stockings.

All around, lights were coming out along the streets. In hundreds of small bedrooms sleepy children woke and groped for presents. They found them too, because we were having our last small boom in shipbuilding, before its rapid collapse in the next few years. The *Duchess of York* was growing slowly under the eagle eyes of the Admiralty, and there were a couple of tankers springing up like mushrooms, that could be called, without a suggestion of irony, *British Honour* and *British Freedom*, forty years ago.

Outside, the pavements rang now with the purposeful

steps of members of alien communions off to their early services, and we smiled drowsily at one another in the pleasant warmth within, feeling rather self-satisfied about our carol-singing and conscious of the varied pleasures of the day ahead, while out across the rimy fields beyond the town, cocks began to crow and under the paling sky lanterned farmers pushed open the byre doors with perhaps that illogical expectation men have had since the first Christmas morning. . . .

Once again the square in front of the baker's shop was the meeting place, and there was again a little warmth and a comforting smell of bread coming up through the grid, and I was glad of it because it was a bitter cold morning. Ten years had elapsed since I had last gone carolling, and the excited grammar schoolboy was now a melancholy young man obsessed with poetry and theology, and, like most of his fellow townsmen, out of work.

The sun shone on the empty stretch of road, and every now and then a cloud blew across it, and there would be a momentary flurry of snow, hardly enough to whiten the hollows between the cobblestones. One or two children passed with new dolls' prams or fairy-cycles from the handful of posh roads south of this corner where I stood.

Northwards towards the river there was silence, although it was eleven o'clock on Christmas morning, except for St. Mark's single bell tolling for matins. There would be a handful of people there, I supposed, but it wouldn't include me, nor Ben, Jimmy and Dave, who I could see converging on me from Albert, Victoria and Alexandra Roads, which appropriately met at this corner.

I stood waiting for them, stamping my feet in my Jermyn Street shoes. My tie—Charvet, though I didn't know it—flapped in the keen wind, and my raincoat, a rubber-smelling one that had gone limp like worn-out oilcloth, was quite inadequate to keep out the cold.

The wind was east and the sea only four miles away. We were going to walk to it this morning. 'A Walk In Winter', I thought, remembering a frequent school composition, and was immediately back in the classroom, back in the sickening odour of ink, and the woody smell of my well-chewed pen. Charlie's ginger head would be next to mine, and the shaven pates of Cam and Kye in front. Mr. Charlton would be strolling up and down the gangways, battering boys here and there with a huge hairy fist if they failed to show enough imagination. I was safe, being appallingly fluent, and had been for many a winter walk across the bleak ploughland that separated our Tyneside town from nearby pit villages. Now Charlie was in the Guards, poor chap, and sometimes came home to stalk up and down the main street where most of the shops were boarded up, ogling what girls there were about from under his perpendicular peak. Cam and Kye I often saw in the dole queue, but I hadn't spoken to them since I changed to the grammar school over ten years ago.

'By, wot a posh tie, Barty,' said Ben facetiously, stamping into the square. His was concealed under a white muffler, but he wore a pair of new tan gloves. Jimmy had a new cap—red and white checks—and little Dave some jazzy socks and a gift box of cigarettes in his pocket. We were glad of these. They would take us through the day. Tobacco was a great consolation, one of the few we had, living as we did on seventeen shillings a week. Not one of the four of us had worked at our trades for over two years. This walk in winter was one of scores taken in all directions, except north. There the river lay, and the silent deserted berths, once full of ships, the empty workshops and the cranes we could see high above the roofs, black and motionless against the cold Christmas Day sky.

Some men never got farther than the lane ends. They squatted on their hunkers against the wall, day after day. There weren't any this morning, though. We were almost the only people about. A few ragged children ran to corner shops for milk and firelighters. They weren't barefoot any more, unless their parents had pawned their Mayor's Boot Fund footwear for food or drink. In most windows hung some sort of mistletoe. I don't mean the kiss-provoking kind. Our mistletoes were wooden barrel hoops wrapped in greenery, from which glass baubles and tinsel were suspended. They were a Christmas-tree substitute.

Apart from this there were no external signs of Christmas, except broken glass in the gutters, and down the candlelit incense-smelling nave of the Catholic church the familiar tableau of the stable at Bethlehem. We just saw it as we passed, but wouldn't have dreamed of going in. Small-town people stuck pretty rigidly to their own places of worship thirty years ago.

I was now C. of E. (in my restless quest for a faith), Ben and Jimmy Primitive Methodists, and Dave a Baptist, and though we didn't go to church any more, we still retained some of the prejudices of our sects. As we marched down the High Street, however, past the whitewashed cottages where beshawled old Irishwomen lived, and saw the squat Norman tower and broken walls of Bede's monastery, all our sectarian feelings were swept away in a glow of pride in our local saint, who transcended, as saints would, all our small-town bigotries.

Seeing the monastery reminded me rather disagreeably of the previous night. I had gone to my own church for once, drawn back partly by curiosity to see the bishop who was coming to preach. The church had been crowded by the time My Lord ascended the pulpit, and an atmosphere of expectation had built up. We were decent poor, clinging to our faith in difficult times. Christmas would have little enough of stage-coach and inn-fire revelry in homes often well below the poverty line. At least our shepherd would, we hoped, give us some words of comfort and hope.

But he didn't. The small figure with its aquiline features waited with studied patience until every cough and shuffle had ceased. He then preached a long, fluent, dry sermon about some codex made originally in our monastery and recently purchased for a fabulous sum from the Russians. To men and women who were worried, unemployed, underfed, but still fond and faithful and true, he gave the dry chaff of remote scholarship with ill-concealed patronage. To make matters worse, a poor chap in the choir had coughed, at which he stopped and turned slowly towards him. Eventually the choirman stumbled out, and I left too, with, I'm afraid, a good deal of noise, and a full insolent look at that aloof uncomprehending face under the pulpit light. I was sorry this morning, but not very sorry. I told the others about it as we skirted the Slacks, where snow-topped black baulks of timber lay in the shallow icy water.

'I don't know how you stand the C. of E. Barty,' said Dave. 'Cold Christ and tangled Trinities.'

'It's better than a smarmy handshake on Sundays, and a look the other way when you're in your work clothes,' I said defensively.

'That must have been a while back,' said Ben drily.

The defects of our churches kept us going till we got to Tyne Dock and its resounding railway arches, and were out of the wind for a bit. My feet were beginning to hurt. West End shoes were all very well, but I wasn't used to this pair yet. Aunt Ellen, who was a housekeeper at Eastbourne, sent me all her young gentlemen's cast-off socks, ties and shoes once a year. That was why I'd been able to discard my comfortable much patched boots for these elegant uncomfortable brogues.

After the warm horse-smelling arches we took a short cut through the Arab quarter. I wondered if they kept Christmas. Most of their wives were English-runaway girls from up and down the river. There weren't many people about. Once we heard a mandolin playing a plaintive unusual air behind a shut café door, and there was a flashily dressed group shivering at the end of the dock wall where we could see the river, grey, empty, and dank smelling. A fruit boat lay at the quay—*City of Delhi* or Calcutta or something. No one stirred on her decks, but a thin whine of 'Good King Wenceslas' came from a wireless set in the galley. Across the empty market square we went, down the long road to the beach.

'I've forgot me bucket and spade,' said Jimmy, and we all remembered our first ecstatic visit years and years before, when we had seen spilt sand on the pavement and with the wild surmise of a crusade had followed its trail in our aching gym shoes down the endless street, past shops and boarding houses until we saw it at last: the grey North Sea.

A wind tore across from the Germany we had been brought up to dread, and we half expected to see a camouflaged cruiser slipping out between the piers, or hear the guns from the fort. Snow powdered the great ruined walls of the cliff-top abbey. Gulls screamed in and out of the flying flakes. We lit some more of Dave's cigarettes and sat with our backs to a convenient rock.

'Howway, let's plodge,' said Jimmy, but we wouldn't. He did, though, slinging his boots round his neck and standing in the hissing foam till his feet were blue. I wanted to try and launch a boat, but Ben wouldn't let me. It was too rough, he said, as we stood waiting for Jimmy to dry himself and making ducks and drakes across the wave tops.

Four miles to come and four to go. And for what? To sit by a cruel sea and watch the waves breaking in fury against the pier and on the ribbed curving beach, where black streamers of seaweed blew out like an uncouth parody of the holly wreaths they'd surely have in those big houses beyond the park where retired sea captains were said to live.

And yet as we rose and stamped our feet, and struggled with the wind and felt (at least I did) the North Sea coming through our shoes, we weren't at all unhappy or depressed. The sea had done something for us. Salt it certainly was, and probably unplumbed and estranging, but as Virgil said, it cleanses the ills of man. I wondered if Ben and Jimmy and Dave remembered. We'd all been at the grammar school together and had odds and ends of the classics knocking about in our minds.

We looked reluctantly back as we crossed the promenade and entered the comparative warmth of the town again. But we couldn't stay any longer. The short day was failing. In the parks, birds were already settling down on the chattering evergreens, and the sun was a dull gold disc behind the tall houses.

'By, I'm not half hungry,' said Ben.

We all were, but there were no cafés open, and if there had been we wouldn't have spent our scant dole money in them. As we went down the sea captains' road a little girl ran across from her garden trying out her new skipping rope. Ben, who was always good with children, pretended to get in her way, skipped in with her a few times, and then took her aside conspiratorially.

'Tell your mother,' he said, like a genial pantomime uncle, 'that there's four poor lads just down the road genuinely seeking work' (that was what they always asked us at the labour exchange) 'and they haven't had a bite all day.'

She gave us a look of horrified compassion and disappeared into a house, where we could see, beyond the lawn and monkey-puzzle tree, a softly lit room lined with books, and the first Christmas tree I'd ever seen outside our parish hall. At the bottom of the road we waited, sitting on the white pillars between which chains were slung to guard this oasis of wealth and culture. It began to snow again.

'Howway, hinneys,' said Jimmy impatiently, 'they'll not let her out again now it's getting dark.'

They did, though. Ben never failed with children. Down the road she came, breathless and excited and with a bag of food. I envied the easy way Ben took it and kissed her, and sent her back with our best wishes to her father and mother. Meanwhile Dave and Jimmy were investigating the bag. There were plenty of sandwiches. They were full of delicious meat I'd never tasted before. 'Turkey!' cried Dave, who evidently had. There were mince pies too. We felt very much better as we set off again. My shoes were easier now and the wind was behind us. Jimmy, made generous by the unexpected Christmas fare, stood us a tram ride to Tyne Dock, so we had only a couple of miles to walk. We passed the Slacks again, but the great stretch of tide-covered mud was invisible, and gulls cried in the increasing dark like lost souls. Nothing stirred in the monastery churchyard but the dry dead grass round the few tilted gravestones visible in the light of the one shifty gas lamp by the gate.

From beyond the railway in the packed streets that lay between the station and the river came the thin high sound of children playing. If for most of them the day had been less than they dreamed it had been different from every other day. Even a good dinner was a treat in those years, and presents, though the cost would have to be calculated in more than money, were not quite unknown.

We weren't depressed as we separated after our winter walk. We'd been together and seen the good old sea and in another week it would be New Year and perhaps the shipyard would open again.

'Many of them, Barty,' said Ben in his expansive way.

'Many of them,' we muttered, shaking hands facetiously.

Then I was alone again on my way back to the outer suburbs where the streets were named after admirals and you could smell the hayfields when the wind was right.

But tonight I kept thinking about the sea and how big it was and how it made our problems seem small, and as I remembered the stinging salt and the shining sands and caught, even here, a hint of a sea smell, somehow a delicious illogical happiness began. It was born of hope, and youth, and the power of identifying myself with nature, and the certainty of some ultimate happy future.

Fled is that Music

THERE were lots of pianos in Grenville Street in 1920. Even Uncle Thomas had one. Most of them had been bought in the last year of the war, when wages were high in the shipyards and steelworks, and the Americans were coming over, and victory seemed certain.

There wasn't much else to buy then except drink, and it was the measure of Uncle Thomas's prosperity that in spite of spending all his spare time and most of his money at the Rolling Mill Tavern he had this black shiny piano in the living room. I doubt if there was a finer one in Grenville Street—except Hardings', of course. That was a baby grand, but then Mr. Harding was a trimmer and didn't know what he was worth! Trimmers levelled off the coal in the stokeholds of ships so that there wouldn't be a list to port or starboard. It was hard grimy work, and was governed by mysterious factors like sailing orders and tides, so that you might hear a trimmer clattering past to or from the river at the unlikely hour of 3 a.m. but it was well paid.

I remember the day when Hardings' piano came. There was enough straw blowing about the street to bed down the two dray horses that brought it. The splendid instrument wouldn't go up the staircase (Harding lived in an upstairs house) and eventually they had to take out the bedroom window, build a ramp and ease it in sideways. Maybe it's still there, though I doubt it. When I walked unheralded and unrecognised down Grenville Street one summer day after nearly forty years I never heard any music except from the ubiquitous record-players. Not a single piano tinkled through open windows as they used to do from half the houses then. And there were no children coming out of those glass and chromium doors—so different from the solid wooden ones of my youth (and you could feel that the old houses didn't approve of them) to trot across the park with their shiny pig-skin music cases to Miss Scott's or Miss Hall's for their weekly music lesson. We used to be very impatient until they came back—not the girls—they didn't matter, but the boys. It was such a waste of perfectly good time that should have been devoted to multikitty or marbles or football. Not that many boys really wanted to learn, but as most of their fathers had acquired a piano and they hadn't all got sisters, many of them had to, though it was the cause of much misery.

I never had a music case. I rolled up my *Roland's Tutor*—fourth hand—like a school textbook, and tied it with a bit of bootlace. We hadn't a piano, but Uncle Thomas (he wasn't a real uncle, but one of my father's mates) let me learn on his. After all, he couldn't play, and Aunt Emma couldn't, and they hadn't any children, only animals. My father died soon after the steelworks shut down and he left Uncle Thomas the field glasses that had picked out the glint of Boer rifles miles away across the veldt, because Uncle Thomas had been in the South African War too, and unfortunately he and Aunt Emma both thought it was their duty to allow me the use of the piano. This was partly because my father, though he had only driven a crane across the sky above the Tyne in his later years, came of a musical family. He sang at local concerts and claimed to be a cousin of Sidney Jones who wrote *The Geisha* and *San Toy* and a number of Gilbert and Sullivan sort of light operas. It was felt I might inherit some of my distant relatives' undoubted talent. Of course, I couldn't afford to go to Miss Scott's or Miss Hall's, but my mother found an old lady in Nelson Street who would instruct me for a shilling an hour, which was quite a lot then, especially to her, as she seemed to live in one room (the other two were clean but bare) with little furniture except this piano and a card table, two rickety chairs, a battered chest of drawers and a bed. She was nearly blind and I was tone deaf, so we made an odd and uncongenial couple, but I was afraid of her and the sharp ruler with which she smacked my incompetent hands, so I really did try to learn. She used to stand behind me smelling of old age and mothballs, muttering blasphemous imprecations while I struggled to combine left and right hands. It was usually night and it must have been winter, because I remember the only light came from two dripping candles on their tarnished piano brackets, and the not unpleasant feeling of warm grease congealing on my fingers. After about three months she died and I've never had another lesson since. I can play 'The Bluebells of Scotland', and a little waltz called 'Golden River', and one or two oddments I used to practise at Uncle Thomas's after tea. This practice time always coincided with his later teatime after the works had come out, but he never seemed to mind my noisy discords. In any case, as Uncle Thomas was a compulsive animal-lover, the house was Bedlam, with canaries trilling, cats mewing for scraps from the table, and Nero, uncle's Great Dane, who had to be fettered permanently to the oven door to stop him savaging Aunt Emma, baying as soon as I opened the piano lid.

After he had eaten his fill Uncle would lean against the sideboard, black from the forge except round his mouth where his tea had cleared a pink space, and cheer me through my current piece.

'Bye, you're coming on, son,' he'd say encouragingly, 'Paderewsky had better watch out!'

One day he waited in unusual silence while I fumbled for the right combinations in 'Blake's Grand March' and almost found them. Then he said, 'Can ye come and give us a bit tune next Thursday, son? Mrs. Lister's coming to tea.' He stood twisting his brass-buckled belt nervously in his knotted hands and well he might. If it had been Queen Mary who'd been coming to tea Uncle Thomas couldn't have been more concerned. This Mrs. Lister lived in a big house beyond the park—very nearly out of the roar and clatter of the works. She had a garden with a dovecote on the lawn, a little maid in a cap and apron, and a pony-trap. Her late husband had been a builder, and a row of decent houses facing the pathetic plane-tree plantations inside the south wall of the park were not only a dignified memorial to the last few years of his industrious life but were said to be owned by his widow. In the ordinary run of things Uncle Thomas wouldn't have moved in her orbit, as I doubt if he had been to church since his wedding, if then, and a leek show at the Engineers' Arms was more in his line than a bazaar at St. John's, but his great concern for animals had brought them together in rather strange circumstances. They had met one afternoon in Redburn Road. Mrs. Lister was driving home in her trap when suddenly as she drew abreast of Uncle Thomas, who was walking the opposite way, the pony shied across the road and tried to enter a draper's shop. This wasn't really surprising. Uncle Thomas, a rather small man, was carrying a well-grown young lion cub in his arms. He'd bought it from a bankrupt gypsy offshoot of Bostock and Wombell's Menagerie encamped on a bit of spare ground by a boat landing. It had cost him the best part of a week's wages and Aunt Emma had rebelled at last. Usually mild and submissive, she had fed and cleaned the birds, looked after the cats and their numerous progeny, and pushed Nero's meal to him with the point of her umbrella expecting at every moment that his chain would break and she'd be eaten in her own kitchen. But even Aunt Emma drew the line at lions.

'Oh no, Tom!' she had cried for probably the first time in her life, and poor Uncle Thomas had found himself outside with the door clashed in his face. What he'd have done if he hadn't met Mrs. Lister I don't know. He had some vague idea of walking out into the country and giving the cub its freedom somewhere in the dreary farmlands between our town and the next. That energetic lady solved all his problems however, and when the trap had been repaired and the young lion despatched to Belle Vue Zoo in Manchester, a curious friendship, based on a mutual love of animals, sprang up between Uncle Thomas and Mrs. Lister. He was always trotting across the park of an evening to see her about some pet or other. Poor Aunt Emma became quite jealous and muttered darkly about some people getting above their station. Then one day

Mrs. Lister announced that she was coming to tea and to see his animals. As only a few weeks before her old groom-cum-gardener had died, we all knew she was considering Uncle for the job. Now the steelworks, soon to close down, was slack in 1920. The Army was on the Rhine and there was relative peace in Europe. The 'shell shop', as we called the ammunition factory we passed on the way to school, had closed already, and its machines rusted in the rains that poured on them through the leaky roofs. Uncle Thomas would soon be out of work and a lot depended on Mrs. Lister's continued goodwill. That was why Uncle Thomas was asking me to add a little culture, or at least what we would now call background music, to what promised to be a nerve-racking occasion.

Aunt Emma cleaned the little four-roomed Grenville Street house from top to bottom, washed the best china, ran up a new pair of lace curtains, and sat down in trepidation to wait. I practised up my few pieces and mother sponged my Eton collar and made me a new bow—blue, of course, a colour that we felt Mrs. Lister would find both aesthetically and politically satisfying. We seemed all set for what we felt would be a successful occasion, when that very morning a letter, ominously typed, arrived for Uncle Thomas. My uncle was in many ways a conventional man. Drink wasn't one of his failings, but gambling was. Aunt Emma was philosophical about it. After all, she said, it might have been both. But he couldn't help putting his money on whippets and race-horses—it was a kind of extension of his love for animals. Surprisingly, Aunt Emma aided and abetted him in this.

'Don't be beat, hinney—take the rent,' I often heard her say when all else had gone. Fortune, however, is fickle, debts mounted up, and callous landlords write curt letters saying that the broker's men are coming for the furniture. They neither know nor care that Mrs. Lister is coming to tea, and they always take objects of luxury first. They were coming for the piano that very afternoon.

Uncle Thomas saw his hopes of making a good impression and getting a safe job blown sky high. Mrs. Lister knew that he had a piano, of course—he'd boasted about it as though it were a Bechstein—and she professed to love music and was looking forward to hearing his so-called nephew play. My own feelings on hearing the dire news were mixed. I was glad to avoid, what I had felt would be an ordeal, but looked forward to the half-crown I hoped might be my reward. Mrs. Lister, when in a good mood, was well known to be a lavish tipper.

'What are ye going to do, Tom?' cried Aunt Emma, actually wringing her hands. He shook his head. Hope, which had sprung so illogically but eternally in Uncle Thomas for so many years, seemed to have died at last. Slowly and sadly he finished bathing Nero. The great dog stepped delicately out of the tin bath that all three of them used, fluffed up his fine fawn hair, and lay down by the warm oven.

Over a reviving cup of tea we considered the possibilities. They were few. I was sent with an extra big bet for the two-thirty, but even Uncle Thomas didn't expect an eleventh-hour miracle to be worked just for him. It was no good going out. The broker's men would only sit on the step until someone returned. If they came before tea we would just have to brave it out with our distinguished visitor and invent some reason for the piano's absence, and if they came after tea it wouldn't matter.

What none of us dared think about was what would happen if their visit and Mrs. Lister's coincided, and, of course, that is exactly what did happen.

Promptly at ten minutes past four we heard her pony-trap draw up outside. There was a thumping of hoofs as Polly, the Welsh cob, came across the pavement to take the carrot Aunt Emma fearfully proffered, and we heard Mrs. Lister's kindly but authoritative tones detailing some street urchin to hold the pony's head for the next hour. You could still earn odd coppers doing this just after the Great War. I had done it myself from time to time, nervously holding the slack of the reins and keeping well away from the white-showing eye and snapping teeth that any self-respecting horse of mettle showed for one so patently nervous of him.

Up the stairs came Mrs. Lister, wheezing and creaking slightly, smelling of lavender water and expensive gloves, and proceeded by a fluttering Aunt Emma in her silk blouse and gold pendant. Her approving glance took in the best china, the shining grate, Nero, tethered, but in his pristine splendour, the well-brushed cats, the canaries in their sanded cages, and me, with clean knees, and liberally scented hair. She had just settled down in Uncle Thomas's one comfortable armchair and leaned back benignly against the cushions, covered with Aunt Emma's best and brightest anti-macassar, waiting till the tea mashed gently on the hob, when there was a dreadful hammering on the back gate, and a raucous tipsy voice shouting, 'Your piano or your life!'

Fortunately the animals were making such a pre-tea-time din that either Mrs. Lister didn't hear or else dismissed it as some unfamiliar street-cry. Poor Aunt Emma's hands shook as she poured out and passed the thin bread and butter. Muttering an unintelligible excuse, Uncle Thomas ran down the back stairs. I followed him. They were there, all right—bowler hats, shabby suits, handcart and all. Moreover, they had been drinking and were full of foolish bonhomie. They whipped off their greenish bowlers and bowed ceremoniously to Uncle Thomas. They did it again, with less reverence, to me. Then, putting us gently but firmly aside, they made to go up the back stairs. With a strangled cry Uncle Thomas ran up a few steps and spread his arms across the stairway.

'Give over, hinney,' cajoled the bigger man, 'don't take it to heart.'

'We're only doing our job,' said his mate, a small man like Uncle Thomas, apologetically.

'Can ye not wait half an hour?' hissed Uncle Thomas desperately. 'I've got company to tea!'

'Tea!' said the little man plaintively, listening to the cups rattling in Aunt Emma's terrified hands, 'I could do with a cup of tea. What about it, hinney? Just give us strength to shift the piano. Like Samson,' he added irrelevantly and incorrectly. He winked at me and spat on his none-too-clean hands. But Uncle Thomas was staring as if he were hypnotised at a ribbon the big man wore in his lapel. I looked at it too. It was like the one Uncle had on his South African war medal upstairs, like the one on my father's which we kept in a tin chocolate box sent (personally, I thought then) to my father by Queen Victoria. Uncle indicated the man's grubby decoration with a trembling finger.

'Who were ye with, hinney?'

The big man looked bemused, then squinted down at his lapel.

'Buller,' he answered.

'So was I,' cried Uncle Thomas. '2nd West Yorks.'

'Northumberland Fusiliers,' said the big man, 'Laing's Nek, Mafeking, Ladysmith . . .'

'Magersfontein, Pretoria, Tugela Heights!' finished Uncle triumphantly, seizing his hand.

'I'm dying for me cup of tea,' said the little man sadly. He hadn't a medal ribbon, and felt left out.

'Give us yer duts,' said my uncle, taking their bowlers. He put them in the pantry on top of Aunt's bread crock.

'Comrades-in-arms, that's what ye are,' he explained conspiratorially, 'come to look up an old swaddy.'

'We'll do owt to oblige,' said the ex-fusilier amiably. 'Tea first. Music later!'

'I was never in the Boer War. I was still at school,' murmured the little man apologetically as we went in, but no one heard him.

'Two more cups, Em,' bawled Uncle, carried away by his ingenuity. 'Meet Mrs. Lister, lads!'

'How do you do?' enquired that lady graciously.

'What cheor, missus,' spluttered the little man, losing his head completely. The big man bowed from the waist.

'I'm champion, lady. How's yourself?' he said.

He sat down and took command of the situation. In five minutes he'd got the general idea that we were entertaining someone important, and was chaffing a scarlet Aunt Emma, joking in a slightly different voice with Mrs. Lister, fondling Nero, and covering up his partner's inept remarks.

'Dick got a touch of the sun at Spion Kop,' he explained.

'Never been the same since, have ye, son?'

Dick shrank with mute embarrassment until he was half under the table.

'Tom was me mate from Cape Town to Jo'burg, lady. I owe it to him as I'm here today. Boer sniper got us and I was bleeding to death on the veldt. Vultures were just about to land. Without the word of a lie, Tom come out under fire and carried us in. They'd have given him the V.C. but there wasn't an officer present. They were aal dead.'

Mrs. Lister's incredulous but amused glance went from the big broker's man to small Uncle Thomas.

'Let's have some music,' said Aunt Emma quickly.

'It's what we come for, missus,' said the little man, bobbing up from under the table, and reckless after four cups of tea. His mate clapped a great hand surreptitiously over his mouth and he subsided again.

In spite of the atmosphere of reckless intrigue and excitement, I got through my two little pieces quite well, and even gave them 'The Robin's Return' for good measure. I'd just finished when there was a knock at the door. Aunt Emma pulled the string that opened it from above, and the urchin called up the stairs that he had to go to take his da's bait to the steelworks and would it do if Cyril held the pony? As Cyril was only four, the party had to break up. We all bowed Mrs. Lister down the stairs and into the trap. On the way she asked Uncle Thomas very cordially indeed to come and see her at ten o'clock the next morning, and he and Aunt Emma exchanged significant and satisfied glances. She also slipped me two bright half-crowns.

'Oh you shouldn't,' said Aunt Emma delightedly.

'Let's call it entertainment tax!' cried Mrs. Lister gaily, giving Polly her head, and away they went, the trap bouncing over the cobbles like a ball.

Off went the piano too, a few minutes later, leaving a big patch of pink wallpaper, a line of waving cobwebs and a long-lost snap of Nero as a pup.

'Fled is that music,' I thought ruefully (we were doing Keats's odes at school), but no one else seemed to mind at all.

The broker's men did Uncle Thomas proud right to the end. They took it down the back stairs and out into the lane. It was a little difficult to manœuvre and an interested group of women and children collected to see the last of the piano.

'Worra shame,' someone observed sympathetically.

'Just taking it in for tuning,' admonished the big man loudly, 'we'll be back next week, hinneys.'

They were too, but it was to take the wardrobe.

On a Dark Night

ALL through July there was a pleasant sense of impending holiday. It triumphed over the daily miseries of mental arithmetic, lay submerged through the annual three-day horror of exams, and reappeared in the last easy-going week when cupboards were cleared, playtimes wonderfully extended, and we read or dozed our way through long warm afternoons, watching the shadow of the school flagpole move across the broken asphalt of the empty yard.

It was, however, a negative sense of well-being, a looking forward to mere freedom from school. Any expectation of a real going-away holiday was confined to the staff and to one or two rich boys like Gordon Emerson, whose father was an undertaker, and Herbert Benson, the only child of a corner-end grocer. The rest of us would only exchange school for street, and there was even a very slight feeling of regret when the Blackie's Model Readers were collected for the last time, and having raced through the Lord's Prayer and sung Grace we poured out of the playground gate at twelve o'clock on a Friday morning, free for four long August weeks.

There was a certain cynicism among us older boys. We observed the screaming seven-year-olds, drunk already on the heady wine of freedom, with amused contempt.

'Where are ye going for your holidays?' someone would ask.

'Kerbside Edge,' was the ritual reply, but Harry Robson made history one summer with the inspired remark, 'I don't know whether to go to Italy or Whitley, man!'

And I remember thinking that to most of us ten-mile-away Whitley Bay with its golden sands and exotic Spanish City was not really much more accessible than Rome itself.

Harry had been no farther than Newcastle, and that only once. I had walked it with him the previous summer —seven long miles each way in aching sand-shoes with nothing to eat but two penn'orth of pigs' trotters, bought where cobbled Bottle Bank twisted its way down to the Tyne a decade before the royal coach trotted triumphantly over Dorman Long's new bridge.

But such excursions were rare, and we could easily count on our fingers the memorable times we had been anywhere, for north beyond the railway, the town, and the clanging shipyards the river ran, deep, wide, and dirty. I used to think how miles and miles away to the north-west it would be a brown burn that a shepherd could leap from heather to heather, but here ferry-boats plied over to riverside towns as drab as our own, and we seldom crossed it. Only the south lay open, and when there was a wind in those long August weeks it brought the smell of hay into town, a nostalgic odour that made us homesick for the country we'd mostly only read about. I used to breathe it in standing on our doorstep in the twilight, catching a whiff now and then through the horsy street smells and the hot reek of slag that came from the heap standing high and square over us like a miniature Table Mountain, and erupting day and night like a harmless volcano.

If you climbed to the top you could look much farther south and see real trees—not the pathetic park hawthorns, too weak and small to be worth climbing, but noble elms where rooks circled and called. We tried to walk there once, but having descended from our vantage point we went in the wrong direction and found nothing more interesting than another colliery village where small men crouched over creased copies of the *Sporting Man* and shivering whippets snarled at our approach.

So we were mostly confined to the streets. I don't know if it was being smaller and closer to the ground, but I seemed to be much more familiar with roads and pavements and their textures and patterns than I am now. Then I knew every slab of cement from our door to the corner shop, all their cracks, markings, and gradients, every cobble and drain and depression in a hundred variegated yards. If you had shown me an aerial photograph I could have said: 'That's Grenville Street—just opposite Charlie Graham's!'

We lived on those hot pavements, stretched full length in the burning sun. At the gutter side small fry in single filthy cotton garments made dust pies with cup and spoon. Cats squirmed in and out of ventilators, and outside each door, except those of a few shiftless sluts, a semicircle of clean pavement steamed to dryness every morning. From the top of the street, where there was a piece of waste ground waiting to be built on, you could just hear the clink of boody as the girls prepared their shops of many-coloured glass.

Sometimes we picked our way through the green yellow and brown patterns, wishing the bits of glass were the sweets they counterfeited, but the bent absorbed girls took no notice of us. It would be September and the dark nights —ages away yet—before they would play with us in the yellow radiance of our gas lamps.

I expect that the weather then was as variable as it is now, but I seem to remember only the dramatic contrasts of blazing sun and sudden thunder rain coming down 'heavens hard' as we say, though each day contrived to have its own atmosphere.

On Monday the poor sheep and cattle went by, pathetic diminishing bands, pursued by ragged children and dogs from one butcher's shop to another until all were penned up hungry and waterless to await Tuesday. This was killing day, when blood poured out under back-shop doors and the sense of death about the town was almost palpable to a child. I was glad when Wednesday came even though it was depressing—like a little Sunday, because the shops shut and you could see yourself in their windows against drawn dark-blue blinds. Thursday brought the Co-op orders on a flat cart drawn by a patient shire mare called Dolly, who stamped over pavements and up to front doors in search of crusts proffered by nervous housewives. There might be bacon for tea, or the chance of a chocolate biscuit. Friday was spent in languishing for Saturday's pocket money. It was a dreary day when we were at our lowest ebb.

Life began again on Saturday as we ran our messages, fetched coal in roaring hundredweight barrows, and bread in big clean pillow cases. In the afternoon we queued to see Elmo Lincoln and Tom Mix in the black orange-smelling and flea-ridden Kino Cinema. Two hours of high adventure later we staggered home in the blinding late afternoon light to lie on the pavement again under the tarred gable end where the Bass advertisement was, and the last remnants of the Kitchener recruiting poster pointed a bleached finger at us.

'Me da says he was drownded,' said Billy Calder, for we often talked about the war and tried to remember the Zepp raids, but mostly we were remembering what we'd been told. I used to tell them about the Somme summer when I'd lain awake in my grandmother's Surrey cottage and heard the doomed men go by.

'I wonder if ye saw me Uncle Bob,' Harry always asked, 'he had a ginger 'tache.'

I might have, but we couldn't check up on it. Like so many others, he never came back.

The war still dominated our thoughts, and under our boyish high spirits we often felt a bit guilty for being alive, and sometimes gave the new cenotaph, with its Latin that would have been Greek to our fathers and brothers, a surreptitious salute as we trotted by.

How terrible the isolation of a wet day was. I used to watch the pool opposite our front window for the first sign of stillness that meant that the rain had stopped. Then out, heedless of my mother's admonitory cries, into the fresh evening world of gleaming stones and full gutters. Our boats, frail as Rimbaud's '*bateau ivre*', raced along to the devouring drain, and if it began to rain again we huddled in someone's front passage—between the street door and the multi-coloured lace-curtained one made mostly of glass a few feet inside. 'Howway in wor passage,' was a welcome invitation from the half of us who lived in downstairs houses. The others had no passages, only stairs rising into mysterious darkness where all the families' coats hung at the stair head. When you knocked for a friend an unseen hand often operated a string that opened the door and you shouted your request up into invisibility.

No one ever let us play on a staircase, except my mother, who was too diffident to remonstrate even when we slid down the steep uncarpeted stairs on a tea-tray.

We seldom really left the street, apart from going on our messages or across the small burnt-up park to Sunday school. Some of us, like the Rutherfords, were forbidden to. Even Bede's Well, less than a mile away under the lee of the slag-heap, was banned to them. I can't think why. The stream that fed the saint's well was never more than a few inches deep, and the fields it meandered through contained nothing more dangerous than a few shorthorns and an occasional straggle of pit-ponies if the Rising Sun happened to be on strike.

Once they defied fate and came with us, but before we'd got our shoes off to plodge in the cressy burn Mrs. Rutherford had appeared over the brow of the potato field, hair streaming, boots unlaced, fists clenched, and after one horrified look Cora, Jim, Peter, and Nessie started for home before their screamed names reached them.

One morning Harry wrinkled his rather runny nose and smelled open water.

'Let's go to the boat-landing,' he said.

This was daring. The place had been forbidden to one and all since Jim Walker had disappeared a year before.

'Howway,' coaxed Harry, seeing our doubtful looks,

'say you're going to Bede's Well, get what bait you can, and be back here for ten o'clock.'

Most of us managed to reassemble—except the Rutherfords, of course.

We had various oddly shaped parcels of sandwiches and medicine bottles of water. There were one or two red and white bait hankies and I had a much washed limp white haversack. We were all in sand-shoes except little Sam, who had to show off and was barefoot.

Harry's strategy was to leave Grenville Street by the southern exit, which would make it look as if Bede's Well was our objective, then double back down Nelson Street and get on to the main road unnoticed. We accomplished this at the cost of a slight scuffle with the Nelson Street boys who objected to us using their territory as a thoroughfare, and soon we were trotting through the warren of narrow alleys round the Rising Sun. Washing hung across the front streets, whippets and babies sprawled in the summer dust. Round the fish-cart pit-wives stood, red hands on bulging hips, shrieking with bawdy laughter. There was a smell of stew and new bread and other people's houses. 'Howway back,' said little Sam, suddenly homesick, but we jeered at him and pressed on towards the river, which was now visible just beyond the high glass-topped dock wall above which we could see the white deck-houses of a 'City' boat.

The river noise was deafening, and a brown haze of dust filled the air. Men in blue overalls passed, carrying mysterious lengths of piping, pungent with new paint. In one or two windows crooked cards hung, advertising good beds for seamen.

At last we found the right turning for the boat-landing

and hurried down the long streets where the Ship and the Golden Fleece were opening, and we could see a flash of brass in the cool gloom and hear the barmaids saying to one another, 'By, it's a lovely day, a lovely day!'

The boat-landing was a floating wooden structure about fifty yards out in the river. There was a tarry open space like a ship's deck, a small stone lavatory like a Gothic shrine, two bollards and a rail over which old and unwanted men leaned and spat into the blue water. Over on the Northumberland side were shipyards and a black tracery of cranes, steep ascending streets where washing flapped, and above them a faint line which might have been Cheviot or just clouds.

The ferry-boat came in and made fast, smelling of oil and stagnant water. An engineer emerged from his domain, squatted in the shade of the funnel and lighted a short clay pipe. A handful of people strolled down the gangway and straggled off up Ferry Street.

We sat with legs dangling over the side and ate our bait. Greedy gulls trod the air for the few fragments of jammy crust, and the wash from a passing tanker made the landing rise and fall like a ship. I was lost in a dream of palm trees and creamy surf and chattering monkeys when a voice behind me said, 'A penny for your thoughts.' I scrambled up and found myself face to face with Isa Cameron. She was in my form at school, and though we'd only exchanged a few words about a mislaid homework book, each of us hoped and half knew that the other cared. Now she stood before me, immaculate in blazer and blue linen. I thought of Venus rising from the sea in the encyclopaedia, and felt myself blushing.

'I've just come off the boat,' she said severely, as though

reading my thoughts. I remembered that she lived on the Northumberland side of the river.

'What are you doing on our side?' I asked, dropping my haversack, which promptly parted company from one side of its frayed strap.

'I'm going to tea with me auntie in Holly Street,' she replied, picking up the haversack before I could.

'Hold still!' she commanded, and, taking a green ribbon from her hair she kotted it neatly to both sides of the broken place. Our hands touched as she meant they should.

Sam and some of the others were making kissing noises and shouting, 'Who's your tart, Barty?'

Isa tossed her head at them and all her black hair spread out like a silky net on the afternoon breeze.

'I won't half get wrong for losing me ribbon,' she said accusingly, but she laughed as she ran up Ferry Street. We met again in the autumn, and I have kept the ribbon (you wouldn't know what colour it had been now) for forty years.

Back we went to the street, where we found we hadn't been missed, to lie with the warm evening sun on our bare legs, our sand-shoed feet aching and water from someone's backyard tap tasting exquisite. The works clamoured all day and every day until five o'clock, when the mournful street-singers were drowned by a flood of iron-shod workmen; only on a Sunday could you hear larks from the far-off fields and the single bell for eight o'clock service and fancy you were near the country.

One day there would be a familiar notice on all the hoardings, slapped across the lurid last-week faces of John Gilbert and Dolores Costello.

'School reopens on September 1st, when every child will be in his place.'

That was a Dickensian touch. If you weren't, the board-man would come and drag you through the streets to the hated building with its cracked bell.

We didn't have to be dragged though, especially those of us who were at the grammar school with its milder rule. One morning we put on unfamiliar boots and blazers again, and ran off through a morning fancied already to be a little chill and autumnal, to the noise, and the reek of ink and acrid leaf bonfires, to write the inevitable defeating essay—'How I spent my holiday.'

'Cheer up, Barty,' said Fred without much conviction as we struggled with this popular but difficult literary form—our models being Lamb, Montaigne and Bacon (not especially helpful to fourteen-year-olds). 'Cheer up, son,' he reiterated, 'it'll soon be the dark nights.' And it soon was. Evening after evening merciful dusk came earlier until it was dark before we were called in from play. Winds, never still long in the north, began to blow, not really cold yet, but with a chilly suggestion of winter now and again. Chrysanthemums drooped in fading front gardens on Fred's estate. In our street, where no living thing ever grew except an occasional blade of grass between the cobbles, there were actually leaves—brown and red and gold like the nature books at school said. I picked them up and pressed them between the pages of Lord Byron's poems and Mrs. Beeton, wondering where they could have come from. The park seemed the likeliest source—it was only five minutes away, but I preferred to picture them coming on Shelley's west wind from the south—somewhere beyond Boldon Hill where I'd never yet been. And when I lay in bed looking at the changing patterns of light and shade our street lamp made on my bedroom wall, and heard the faint rasping of leaves along the pavements, I felt the suffocating boundaries of the town dissolving and its summer-long insipidity dispelled by those twin agents of darkness and wind.

Autumn and the dark nights did not mean that there was any less playing out of doors. With no television, and wireless in its infancy, we 'ran the streets', to use my mother's contemptuous phrase. I suppose a few namby-pambies disappeared for the duration to fiddle with fret-work and read piles of accumulated comics, but to most of us it made no difference. The lamp, conveniently situated outside our front door, was a rendezvous for everyone, and by six o'clock on a fine night there must have been twenty children competing for its shifting circle of yellow radiance.

No one played at the other lamp farther down the street outside Mrs. Croft's. That was an unhappy house, one of many made miserable by drink and unemployment. There were two girls, Maud and Mabel, shabby silent creatures who sometimes played with us. They were always chosen last in games. On bitter midwinter nights, when Fred and I were returning from some long walk, we would often see them, huddled in an amorphous mass on their door-step, saying 'What cheer!' with defensive brightness as we passed and hoping we hadn't heard the dreadful bumps and angry voices from upstairs.

The third lamp we never thought of as being in our street at all as it was a hundred yards beyond the last house on the edge of the field, as we called the brick-strewn couple of acres between us and a farm, and early in the evening while there were still people about we sometimes played there. You could see the whole black bowl of sky brilliant with stars except where the immense bulk of the slag-heap blotted it out.

Its own lunar landscape, made from a whole century's furnace waste, was illuminated punctually every hour by two blazing eruptions of molten slag. On a still night you could hear not only the frantic puffing of the steelworks train that took two ladles up to the top of our mountain, but the clink of couplings and even the warning shouts of driver and fireman at their glamourous, fearful task.

One night we made an expedition to the slag-heap. It was the year Isa Cameron crossed the water and came to live briefly in our street. This was a few months after our encounter on the boat-landing, the autumn of 1925. I am sure of that because I'd bought a little book of Edgar Allan Poe's poems at Geordie Conway's second-hand shop in Grange Road, and I still have it.

I used to rummage there every Saturday with my penny pocket money while Geordie chewed his dirty yellow moustache and watched impatiently in case I pinched any of his shabby stock of Nat Gould's and W. J. Locke's. Because the poetry book was small (Geordie tended to sell books like furniture by size) I got Poe for a penny. He was heady stuff.

Fred and I learned 'The Bells' and 'Annabel Lee' and we chanted them wherever we went. I couldn't open the coal-house door without intoning ' 'Tis the vault of thy lost Ulalume,' much to my mother's irritation.

Tennyson was her favourite poet because she had once been a nursemaid in his household, and she thought Poe silly and decadent, with his preference for night over day, and his predilection for the mysterious and macabre.

All that autumn Fred and I read and re-read the little green book and tried to invest our everyday North Country streets with some of Poe's sinister magic, so that it was only natural that when Isa Cameron came we should transfer it to her.

She was from 'over the water', which sounds romantic and Jacobite but merely meant the Northumberland side of the Tyne—Wallsend in fact, where Hadrian's defensive fortification against the marauding Picts was supposed to conclude its seventy miles of serpentine wanderings from the sea beyond Carlisle. Her slightly different accent, her good looks, and the fact that she came to live in one of the very few self-contained houses in our street, put her in a class slightly above the rest of us. She proved to be a natural leader too, and soon Winnie, Edna, Ethel and Olive—and, of course, the silent unregarded adoring Crofts—were dancing attendance on her.

We boys affected not to care, but whatever independent game we began somehow she drew us into her orbit and we found ourselves half-unwillingly dominated.

I can see her now, pale and dark, with a Rossetti mouth, wearing some short awful fur coat from which her long perfect legs emerged in their flesh-coloured stockings. My mother was disgusted. Fred, just getting girl-conscious, adored them. I was above noticing legs in his profane way, but I looked at her face and in a week I was desperately in love. In fact we all were, Fred and me and Henry and Albert and Alf—even little Sam whose thoughts had never risen above footer and marbles before.

The street that autumn seemed full of Isa. She was out at all hours running over the fields, crowding round

Handyside's diminutive shop window to guess what 'S.L.' meant, and then, when someone shouted 'Soda Lunch!', tearing breakneck to Carr's grocery store with its greeny light from half a gas mantle. It was possible to touch her sometimes in a running game, or perhaps she took your hand to hurl you into the road when we played 'Statues'. Those were thrilling moments. I was reluctant to wash the hand that had been so honoured, so it was fortunate that such contacts were rare.

In spite of her former predilection I seemed to have no chance of 'going with' Isa, as we say. Nor had Fred. She changed her lovers as often as she changed her frocks, but the athletic and the forceful (Henry and Albert) were her obvious choices, and we, alas, were neither.

Fred might call her his 'Rare and radiant maiden', and I might, greatly daring, implore her (from the safety of fifty yards' distance) to 'Take me to thy bosom fair', but neither of us expected more than an occasional smile.

As for the kisses that Henry boasted about in an off-hand manner, they could only be 'By hopeless fancy feigned', as Lord Tennyson had it. Until the night we climbed the slag-heap, that is. Of course, it was Isa who suggested it. She was always ready for nocturnal adventures. With her we had already been to the haunted house in the brickfield, said to have been the refuge of German spies, and crouched among its crackling undergrowth to watch a candle moving from room to room inside. When a door banged we had all fled except Fred, who feared nothing. He joined us later round the lamp, swearing something had chased him as far as Granny Grieves's bread shop—with a knife, he ventured, not being used to the luxury of an audience, but we wouldn't quite accept that.

However, Isa chose him first in 'Leavo' and paid him marked attention all evening, so he had his reward.

We were so excited about this night visit to the slag-heap because anywhere out of the street and in the dark was exciting, and also it might offer someone else a chance to show courage, which was one way to Isa's favour.

I thought I had found another more subtle way, and it was with delicious dread that I watched her take from time to time a sheet of stiff school paper from her bosom (those were the days of silent films) on which I had written a poem declaring my love.

'Had I but known the sorrows love would cost me; the burning cheeks, the flushed and heavy eyes', it began. I know, because the rough draft is still here in the front of Poe's poems. I wonder if Isa still has the fair copy?

As we went up the farm-track to the slag-heap we chattered like starlings. It was a dark night, windy and cold. I looked rather longingly back at Grenville Street where I could just see the lamp and Maud and Mabel Croft swinging slowly round it on a skipping rope. Across an inky turnip field where Fred and Alf were foraging with their Scout knives were the new electric lamps on the high road to Newcastle and beyond that the river lights, blinking in the wind. Some on the tall invisible cranes seemed as high as the stars. In one of those odd moments when everybody stopped talking you could hear near at hand the comfortable breathing and stamping of horses in their stable, the clang of a steel plate being dropped in a shipyard two miles away, and, faint and thin, the voices of children playing in the streets of Wallsend over in Northumberland.

Soon we were off the farm-track and on the hard furnace-made rock, the slag itself. The lower slopes of this mountain were familiar to most of us by day, but night made each crag boulder and cave a menacing presence.

When we stopped, other footsteps seemed to be climbing towards us. An owl glided by, near enough to touch, and we heard his long cry blown back to us from the fields below. What we didn't hear, because we were too familiar with the sound, was the steelworks engine puffing its way to the top on the other side of the slag-heap.

Little Sam's torch showed us our frightened faces. Winnie grinned nervously.

'Ee I'm going home!' she said.

'Then ye can go by yourself!' replied Fred rudely, knowing she wouldn't dare.

'What's that!' breathed Ethel.

'Only the wind,' said Isa, smiling at someone (could it be me?) with her Rossetti mouth. But it wasn't the wind. Someone was running towards us across the slag. We heard a hoarse threatening shout.

'It's Jacka Lacka!' gasped Henry, and at those terror-striking words we fled along the base of the mountain, scrambling over the screes, falling, and getting up, and feeling blood running down our legs. I could hear Edna sobbing and little Sam muttering, 'I've lost me torch, I'll get wrong for losing me torch.'

It was too dark to see anything, and to make matters worse plovers were crying and some farm horses began galloping like thunder in the field below.

I wondered as I ran if it really was Jacka Lacka who was chasing us. He was a shell-shocked hermit who haunted the area, and was said (probably wrongly) to live in a cave there, but the name was applied indiscriminately to anyone of tramp-like appearance.

Suddenly a great wave of warmth enveloped us. I felt it burn right through my clothes. Simultaneously the whole sky grew light—not with the cool light of day, but with a white scorching radiance that poured from above like fire from heaven.

In its unearthly grow we saw one another transfixed in attitudes of flight as if we were playing some involuntary game of statues. Isa was a bare arm's length away from me. A second flood of heat and light poured down and I found I was holding Isa's small hot hand. Her hair was blown across my face by the torrid wind. Then, as the flood of lava cooled, it turned from white to dull red, to black, as quickly as a tropical sunset, and we were in the dark again.

Fred climbed up beyond our position of safety and brought back a piece of barely cooled lava.

'It's like the last days of Pompeii, Barty,' he said. I hardly heard him because Isa had just kissed me. It was for the poem, of course, and it was like her to choose a moment of fear and excitement on this sulphurous slope rather than a doorway or backlane at home.

The stars were all very bright as we went back. In their light we could see the tired horses standing under a bleak row of hawthorns, their manes and tails rising in the wind, and heard Bede's Well bubbling as it rose to feed the streams that crossed the fields. The slag-engine, with its two empty ladles, puffed along at ground level now on the far side of the turnip field—on its way back to the steelworks. Orion, his belt glittering, stood high above us.

There was no sign of Jacka Lacka. Shaken into sanctity

and reminded of the end of the world—Olive swore she had heard Gabriel's trumpet—we talked about God all the way back. It was Fred who silenced us at last.

'What I want to know,' he said slowly, 'is who made God?'

Isa didn't let go my hand until we got to our street again where the Croft girls were slowly swinging as though the last hour had never happened. Eventually we dispersed to do forgotten homework and pacify irate parents. Isa and I hung back by mutual agreement. She kept Winnie back too, and that stolid willing child soon came over from Isa's doorway to mine.

'Isa says, do you go with her?' she asked with uninvolved ease.

'Yes,' I stammered, and watched her cross the street with this brief but momentous answer.

Someone called from an upstairs window, and Isa had to go in, but before she did so I saw her write something on the brick wall. It was just light enough to read it, and a good job that I did, because as I lay in bed I heard a sudden sea wind flinging rain against the gable opposite, and in the morning the three precious words were gone.

It rained all the next week and on the first fine day there was a furniture van at Isa's door and she had gone too—far away to Carlisle, Winnie said—without another word or look.

The dark streets had no more excitement for us that winter. Fred and I gave up quoting Poe and took to leaving the crowd round the lamp and walking along the road that led west to seventy-mile-away Carlisle until we were worn out.

'Did ye see her?' jeered Winnie, whose unrequited love

for Fred had made her perceptive. He soon consoled himself with her, but I thought myself heartbroken all the long winter, until one piercing March day, when the park was full of daffodils and the dark nights were almost over, I turned into our street and there she was, long-legged and lovely as ever, holding her ecstatic court round the just-lighted lamp outside our door.

Sometimes I can feel just a faint reverberation of the fearful joy with which I walked that hundred yards of suddenly golden street.

Enter Will Shakespeare

SOMEONE, a girl I expect, once gave me a 'Shakespeare Birthday Book'. You keep a record of your friends' birthdays in it, and there is a quotation for each date —generally a piece of sententious advice, or some few appropriate words applicable to the season. My own was 'Neither a borrower nor a lender be', and that strikes home with peculiar force because I remember getting into tremendous debt as an office boy, and even having the arrogance to put a notice on the board saying, 'No loans of less than fourpence will be repaid', when I had squared all my major creditors.

Thinking of Shakespeare always makes me think of Castlemain. He was one of the handful of people who have made me what I am—but immediately I write 'handful' I realise it's more than that. I remember a line of Tennyson's—'I am a part of all that I have met,' and that's certainly true for me.

Every time I write, my Greek E's remind me of Miss Andrews, a young English mistress I copied them from. My slight conscious stutter belongs to a handsome and more successful student friend, my occasional (and quite sham) cool arrogance, to an old Etonian met briefly in the army.

I sometimes wonder what, if anything, is really mine. From Castlemain I get my hatlessness in all weathers, my way of lighting a cigarette, a kind of high-shouldered literary slouch (very unbecoming now I am middle-aged) and a love of Shakespeare that without him might have had to wait years for its awakening.

Fred, my *alter ego* for the ten long years of school, got that too, but remained his sturdy forthright Geordie self. He never understood my physical identifications with anyone and everyone I admired, and I would often notice his sardonic grin when I was obviously acting like my current hero or even heroine!

Castlemain was a bird of passage at the grammar school. He taught us English for a few months in the mid-twenties; not too briefly to be unremembered, not so long that his glamour wore off.

There were quite a number of such temporary young men and women during our time there. I suppose they were university students trying out the vocation that teaching is thought to be, or else persons that our head didn't get on with and sent on their way. Casting my mind back, I can remember, apart from Castlemain, only Miss Andrews, on whom I had a thirteen-year-old crush, and a dark nameless girl who taught us French for three blissful weeks. I have never known anyone as beautiful, kind, and remote. She was like the lovely aloof girl in some film who ultimately takes the veil. Once she actually played hockey (borrowing Caroline Norton's gym frock) and it was as if a goddess had descended upon the pitch to emphasise, with quite unconscious cruelty, the Searle-like creatures of the lower fourth.

I would readily have paired her off with Castlemain,

but their times with us didn't coincide. He came in 1926. I remember because it was May, and cold, and we were foraging for fuel just after the General Strike. One morning a tall young man with long untidy hair, grubby flannels, and a peculiar tie came in, holding a copy of *Macbeth* between finger and thumb. He grinned at us and we relaxed after an hour's Latin, and grinned back. I heard Peggy Oliver gasp, but she swooned at practically any male, even old Mr. Hunter who took us for physics and was over sixty.

'This book is dripping with blood!' he said, and dropped it gingerly on the table. Some of us with enough sense took it metaphorically, but one or two simple or deliberately disingenuous souls got up to investigate.

I forgot what Castlemain said next, or indeed what he said at all, but I do remember that when the bell rang and we trooped out into the windy lunchtime field four years' resistance to the immortal bard had begun to melt away.

Most of us had hated Shakespeare and all his works. At my elementary school I had hardly heard of him. This was because Mr. Macdonald, our headmaster was a Scot, and put him second to Burns—a long way second. The Bible came first, of course; we were made to learn long bits out of it, and I can still declaim various chapters of Isaiah and Corinthians. But this was scripture—quite a different thing from poetry. Poetry was always in the afternoon, when the eccentric Macdonald spouted interminable dialect passages and even called on us to read them. There were a certain number of Scots in a Tyneside school, but the rest of us made heavy weather of 'Wee sleekit cowerin' timorous beastie' in strong but unsuitable accents.

As for acting plays, Mr. Macdonald favoured stark moralities like *Everyman*. Fred was very nearly in that; he was Lemon Wardle's understudy for Strength, being big for his age—'Must be all the corned beef I eat,' as he observed—and I was Goods because I was slim and could slip into a chest of imitation money halfway through the first act. It was during all the waiting about that school play production entails that Fred and I became friends rather than acquaintances.

There was a photograph of the cast at the end of our three-day run and I moved and spoiled it. Everyone said it was because I was cross-eyed.

I'm not, but such is the power of suggestion that in my mortification I did think that I was for several weeks, and would peer so earnestly into the looking glass that my father would say with sympathetic misunderstanding, 'Your kindness exceeds your personal beauty.' The repetition of this and other pompous aphorisms is sometimes taken for wit on Tyneside, but not, as I have found since, anywhere else. My only other experience of acting occurred earlier than *Everyman*, and was confined to our classroom. Miss Corrigan believed in dramatising history, and I remember her lifting me up on to her high chair to be King Canute. I can still feel how cold her shining pattens were, right through my sailor blouse. 'Go back, O sea!' I declaimed loudly to the rows of desks and a glass case full of squirrels. Canute may have doubted his power, but I was drunk with it.

Next term I was one of the burghers of Calais with a halter round my neck, carrying a slate with the school keys on to an unkingly blue-suited Edward. We were allowed to take off our boots and stockings for this, and

I remember Fred saying with an early touch of his terse common sense, 'She'd have saved herself time if she'd picked half a dozen paper lads.'

There were still a lot of barefoot boys then, and most of them cried the *North Mail* and the *Evening Chronicle* round the town twice a day.

Shakespeare was practically missed out of our first seven years of school, but Mr. Macdonald showed us a picture of him and made us learn a list of his plays when we went for the interview that formed the third part of our scholarship exam.

He must have had some dim notion that Burns didn't hold pride of place with everyone; and sure enough there was an identical picture on the wall of the head's study where a row of worthy people sat behind tables asking us questions.

I hoped they would say, 'Do you know who this is, my boy?' but having heard me read a page of 'The Lady of the Lake' and asked me the meaning of 'substitute', I was in.

The very first week in Form I Mr. Wilson's unconscious campaign to develop hatred of Shakespeare started. He gave out thin stringy copies of *Richard II*. They were inky and unattractive. Castlemain would have burned the lot out of hand. I believe he did something of the sort, but naturally he got no thanks for it.

We read 'Dick 2', as Mr. Wilson facetiously called him, round the class without even giving people parts—just so many lines each. When we came to a long piece like, 'O who can hold a fire in his hand by thinking of the frosty Caucasus,' we learned it, while Mr. Wilson thankfully went back to his copy of *The Motor Cycle*.

In time, and with various teachers, we memorised a

score or so of famous speeches, but I can't remember that we had the slightest appreciation of them then. I had an excellent memory in those days, and could gain an easy ten marks each week, but though I already read and wrote quantities of poetry, Shakespeare meant absolutely nothing except a weekly task and long dreary class readings with minute-by-minute references to the glossary.

On the credit side it is fair to say that once or twice in the war, left bookless on some desolate rifle range, or caught without my current paper-back during a long wait outside Company office. I have got some pleasure out of going over 'The quality of mercy' or 'This royal throne of kings', and when not quite sober I have an appalling tendency to leap on to the nearest table and declaim 'Henry before Harfleur', but by and large this isn't much to take away from school.

Castlemain's first lesson woke us up to reality. In half an hour Will Shakespeare ceased to be a dry scholar scratching away with his quill in Anne Hathaway's cottage. Most of us had unconsciously identified him with our headmaster, a cold man, all teeth and glasses, a competent botanist I believe, but utterly remote from the savagery and splendour of the Tudors.

Unfortunately he was a Shakespeare fanatic, and Will's lightest word was only a little less inspired than the scriptures. To see him take up a copy of *A Midsummer Night's Dream* or *Twelfth Night*, read a speech, and then explain it, was to see Shakespeare lovingly and slowly strangled.

Next time Castlemain came in we began to act *Macbeth*. Back went the desks to the wall, the three prettiest girls were chosen as witches (Castlemain was full of tact like that) and off we went. It was noisy, improvised, absurd, and utterly delightful. Castlemain was everywhere—now a witch, now the serjeant, now Macbeth—diffident calculating, ambitious—now poor honest Banquo. The bell rang and classes streamed by on their way to other lessons. Miss Mason stood, tight-lipped, in the doorway with a pile of Latin proses under her arm, but we were still on a blasted heath in medieval Scotland.

Fred and I walked home in a rare state of satisfaction with school. It was like knocking up a six or being praised for a dogged game of football. Such euphoria didn't often attend classroom subjects. As we strolled down the long suburban road that late warm afternoon an extraordinary home-made looking motor car shot by, and a voice cried, 'What bloody man is that?' It was Castlemain, of course, tie and hair flying, one leather-patched negligent arm waving. His triumph was short-lived. Halfway down the road the engine gave out, and we had to shove him two hundred yards. I fell and tore my already worn flannels, but Castlemain said the rent wasn't as wide as a church door. 'Nor as deep as a well, sir,' I managed, and got an approving look. 'What did your last servant die of, sir?' asked matter-of-fact Fred in his grudging way: but we'd both have pushed that little two-seater to Timbuktu.

We never knew where Castlemain came from. Oxford and Cambridge had their rival devotees, but his odd tie was never identified. He limped very slightly, and Gladys Gasgoigne said it was a legacy of the Marne, but that had been in 1914 and would make him over thirty which wasn't probable, and in any case Gladys was incredibly romantic—but that was the sort of legend that grew up round Castlemain.

Rumour filled the spare seat in his car with every

eligible sixth-form girl. It was said that he'd taken Carrie Norton to Durham to sketch the cathedral, and Barbara Jones to the Theatre Royal in Newcastle. Irene Gibson, a thirteen-year-old nymphet in IIC, actually dared to sit in his car one day after school, but Castlemain drove her home with complete nonchalance. In fact the laugh was on her. She lived in Western Road down by the steelworks—a terribly *declassé* area, and he insisted on accepting an invitation to a cup of tea from her ma.

Meanwhile the rehabilitation of William Shakespeare went on. Castlemain detested the fat pop-eyed butcher of the usual portrait. It shouldn't matter what people look like, but it does, especially to children, and we took immediately to the mysterious young man in the Grafton portrait that Castlemain and Professor Dover Wilson was sure was Shakespeare. We got to quoting, and not only from *Macbeth,* almost daily and naturally.

This had its penalties. Fred was watching Mr. Tanner puffing down the field from sports practice with IVA and his loud remark about Simon (as we called him from 'one Simon, a tanner,' in the Gospels) 'larding the lean earth', got him a hundred lines from that amiable but vain master.

I don't remember Castlemain teaching us any grammar or language study or anything like that. Occasionally we wrote him an essay. He read some of mine out to the form and said he'd look out for my first book. Perhaps this was a factor in making me a writer of sorts, a willing acquiescence, like his hunch-shouldered walk that I still see myself affecting in shop windows.

I suppose he taught other forms too, though he seemed to belong exclusively to us, Lower V, a form of duds put together because they didn't fit in with the carefully academic tone of the school.

Most of us weren't interested in or capable of school certificate—and you had to get it all in one go then—and were drifting happily through a pleasant respite between the cruel rigours of elementary school and an inevitable five years of apprenticeship in the shipyards.

Perhaps Castlemain's ideas were a bit revolutionary for the staff-room and the VIth, who faithfully reflected their values, and I doubt if he was *persona grata* with the head for long. I think he liked being with us where he wasn't expected to repeat safe judgements and cram us with notes for exams.

At the end of summer term there was an informal school concert. It wasn't at all like Speech Day, which took place in the autumn and was rigidly classical in form. Summer-term concert was a go-as-you-please affair. Every form was expected to contribute something and every form did. With exams over and the sweet prospect of seven weeks' holiday ahead, criticism hardly existed.

In spite of these relaxed standards, our form still seemed to lack any real talent for anything, and when Castlemain coolly announced that Lower Vth were going to do scenes from *Macbeth* there were exclamations of horror. Five days was all the preparation ever allowed. And school was always a Bedlam during that last week. Staff came and went, sitting grimly at their desks in front of us, and scribbling sarcasms in those dreadful red-backed report books that spelled doom to so many. In the music-room pianos were belted by would-be Pachmans. The gym was full of kids doing complicated pyramids. And round and round the school field paced solitary boys and girls like priests and nuns with their breviaries. These were trying to learn poems and parts in plays. With them, the hot sun burning our backs, went Fred and I and Gladys and Peggy, and anyone else who had a part. Fred and I were in Act II, scene I. It's very short: Banquo, Fleance, Macbeth and a non-speaking servant. That was Fred. Banquo was a boy called Jenkins who went down the pit when he left school. Fleance, his son, was Dixie Dean, an extremely neat little boy, suitably small for his age. I saw him years later, driving a taxi in Bristol. I was Macbeth, partly because I'd have done anything for Castlemain and partly because I had the best memory in the form. Unfortunately I didn't look at all like Macbeth. I was a slim stooping boy in crooked glasses, already half-blind without them.

I knew that when I came to 'Is this a dagger which I see before me?' some wit would call out, 'Get your specs on, Barty, and have a look!' Fred had already done so. It was all right for him. All he had to do was stand about holding a torch aloft and 'Get thee to bed' when I told him to. I didn't mind the first part of the scene but I dreaded my longish last speech alone on the stage.

I was soon word perfect—that was easy—and I could prompt the less fluent Banquo and little Fleance, but as soon as they'd gone a dreadful incompetence descended on me. I couldn't feel at all like Macbeth except in being nervous and irresolute.

Fred snatched my dagger impatiently and rolled his eyes like Godfrey Tearle.

' "I see thee still and on thy blade and dudgeon (What's a dudgeon Barty?) gouts of blood, which was not so before." I don't think its all that difficult.'

'You're welcome to it,' I said ruefully, but, of course, he wouldn't change parts.

In fact I'd only seen Fred act once before. Our church had done a passion play at Easter, just before Castlemain came. Fred had to take a part. At first he wouldn't, on the grounds that he couldn't do so conscientiously because he was an atheist like his father. Under pressure he accepted the part of Judas, which for some reason, and much to the vicar's amusement, he thought quite suitable.

I had been Peter, and we'd had a long slanging match after the crucifixion when I had driven him off the stage with, 'Go, wretched man, ere Satan thy master claim thee for his own!'

This time I had to be content with Fred's silent support, but it was something. I was very glad of it as we pushed through the dust-smelling curtains on that blazing July afternoon.

'Screw your courage to the sticking point!' hissed Castlemain in an old khaki shirt (maybe the Marne story was true) and on we went. It wasn't too bad. No one actually forgot a word and no one laughed except at 'the bell invites me' and in a milieu like school punctuated by bells, that was inevitable.

And just for a moment halfway through my speech I *was* Macbeth. It came to me as Castlemain had said it would. I didn't mind the inappropriate sunlight pouring through our awful stained-glass window and the rows of all too visible faces. A voice I hardly recognised as my own was saying, 'Withered murder—thus with his stealthy pace towards his design moves like a ghost.'

I lost it again before my exit, but Castlemain thumped me on the back till I was sore, and I knew that in some way we'd justified his efforts with Lower V.

Next day the holidays began, but they didn't amount to much on Tyneside in the slump years, and long before the seven weeks were up Fred and I were looking through the locked gates where first falling leaves dropped towards their dusty shadows, and waiting impatiently for mid-September.

It came, but Castlemain didn't. We never saw him again. Peggy said he'd gone back to Oxford. Gladys said that he'd quarrelled with the head (who mistook cramming for teaching) and had started a school of his own down south. Someone, on the strength of that khaki shirt, said he'd rejoined the Army. At any rate, he wasn't on the platform among the gowns and new suits. Our corridors were desolate without him.

Miss Lewis took us for English that term. Wordsworth was her favourite. 'The sounding cataract haunted me like a passion,' she intoned earnestly. It didn't do a thing for us. And I've never cared much for the Lakeland poets since. But she had the grace when she saw our stricken faces not to touch Shakespeare for a whole term, and we were all very grateful for that.

Battles Long Ago

IT was always the Great War to us because its scope had dwarfed all previous ones. We never thought of calling it 'World War I'. Such a cynical journalists' title only became common when we were well into the second, and in the twenties when I was at school another war seemed impossible.

Peace, signed in the Hall of Mirrors, and celebrated by the bonfires that burned all night on the slag-heap, had ushered in the millennium. Half Europe might be starving, but the trestle tables groaned with food on the cobbles of our insular streets. Each had its own Victory Tea. Of course, we thought Grenville Street outdid Jervis, and naturally it was in a different category from the wild saturnalia with which Nelson Street celebrated the end of hostilities. But now the good-natured scrambling for cakes and fruit and ham sandwiches was over. A Union Jack or a Tricolour still fluttered here and there, hung in some impossible place not worth climbing up to in our mood of apathy after the feasting was over. In time they would lose their brightness during the winter rains, and perhaps survive, limp and dingy rags, for a year or two.

Our Commemoration beakers, crudely designed and roughly executed, collected dust already on the top shelf of the pantry. It seemed sacrilege to use them. I sometimes took them down and looked at the imperfectly coloured Allied flags and the fateful dates that boys nowadays learn with no more intimate feelings than they have for those of Waterloo or Hastings.

1914–18. To us these were the most significant figures of all time, and even today, half a century later, any one of those five fatal years rings out like the trumpets that soldiers of the Faithful Durhams sounded across our town every Armistice Day. The silence really was a silence then. The Armageddon of shipyard and steelworks was cut off at five to eleven like the gun-fire on the Western Front that first November Monday. Horses were held; buses stopped; suburban trains sought the nearest station. You could hear the unfamiliar sound of sparrows chirping in Western Road by the blast furnaces, and the wind in the stubby plane trees along Ellison Street. We stood tense, not even breathing, behind our desks in school, while the red Autumn sunlight slanted across from the playground where the Union Jack licked the misty morning air. Some of us raised secret adoring eyes to the engraving of John Travers Cornwell, the boy V.C., for ever at his post in the thunder and flame of Jutland. The weight of glory and death was heavy upon us. The heroes were all gone and we were young and guilty and alive. When I read Edmund Blunden's line, 'Why slept I not in Flanders clay with all the murdered men,' that seemed to strike our note.

Life, without the chance of heroism, without the possibility of atonement, stretched out in front of us. This titanic conflict had brought war to an end and the Territorials who still marched off to nostalgic weekend camps were pathetic anachronisms whose time was fast running out.

Our guilty feelings were quite illogical. We weren't born till just before the war, and in that mythical golden summer before the fatal shot was fired in Sarajevo were scarcely conscious of anything beyond the small circles of our families. My father might look grave over the *North Mail*. He'd fought in South Africa and could claim a professional interest in any future conflict, but sitting on my toy-box driving Punch, my beloved wooden horse across the carpet, I never noticed.

Fred, my school friend of later years, claimed to remember the night war was declared. His mother had held him up to see a particularly bright sunset, he said, and he once wrote with great pride in a fifth-form essay: 'The splendid finale of a world now as lost as Atlantis.' But this was years later when we were growing up in the bleak twenties and beginning to be literary and critical.

I can't claim as early a memory as that. I slept through the dramatic night of August 4th in the big whicker cradle and I didn't notice we were at war until 1915.

'Gallipoli' is the word that brings it all back. In that year it was on everyone's lips. To me it was just a strange meaningless sound that went with fists banged on the breakfast table and sad anger. There was no wireless then and we never heard odd names properly pronounced. 'Gally-Polly', everyone said, except perhaps the vicar, and my mother went on saying it obstinately for the rest of her life. It was years before I read about those desperate landings, and by then Brooke's poetry and Masefield's prose had got all mixed up with the pattern on the carpet where I sat with my toys, and the smell of frying bacon and my father raging about this funny sounding far-off place where his old friends' lives were being wasted.

He never really got over not joining up. If he had, as a South African War serjeant-major, he'd have got a commission and gone to France or Salonika or Malta like his brother Uncle Leo, who sometimes came on leave and brought champagne. The cork hit the ceiling and the mark was still there when father died ten years later. But he wasn't very young, his heart even then was imperfect, and his workmates who weren't very pro-soldier foresaw big money in munitions and persuaded him against it. He drove his crane in the steelworks, had his brief prosperity in 1918, and then, like thousands, never worked again. My mother, who was a great patriot, would rather have had him dead and on the cenotaph than the bitter sick man poverty and unemployment made him. He knew she was right. A soldier, and the son of a soldier, he felt he belonged to the war, had been cheated of his birthright, and should not have survived it.

I would often look at this cenotaph as I went to and fro to the shops down the street in the years after the war. It wasn't impressive architecturally—Lutyens and water—but I liked the inscription: 'So they gave their bodies to the commonwealth and received each for his memory, praise that will never die, and with it the noblest sepulchre; not the spot where their bones are laid, but a place in the minds of men.'

It was, and has remained the only bit of Pericles I know, and as I learned it one wet November afternoon while the paper poppies and beribboned wreaths were beaten down to its sad concrete base I wished passionately that my father's name was among all the Armstrongs and Simms and Booklesses, and that I hadn't to go home to the haggard querulous man whom I was ceasing to respect and love.

I suppose I first noticed soldiers at my grandmother's in Surrey. We didn't see many on Tyneside. There were plenty of sailors and thousands of men in overalls, but only an occasional man on leave in khaki. But down at Grandmother's, a mile up the road from her cottage, was one of the biggest camps in England.

The great common, once given over to ling and bracken, was now alive with soldiers. I used to stand under the great chestnut tree (it doesn't seem so big now) by Grandmother's gate and watch them go by—horse, foot and guns. I loved the exciting smells of leather and sweat and horses. The brown young men in shirt-sleeve order and putties and shining boots would wave to me as I clung to the gate if their officer wasn't looking, and I would watch them out of sight in the white clouds of stinging dust that rose and settled on the lower leaves of the green hedges.

'Gone to the front,' my mother said—a perplexing phrase to a five-year-old, but I realised by her gravity and by the way her lips moved in silent prayer that it was somewhere important and dangerous. Across the meadow beyond Grandfather's orchard was the railway from London to Portsmouth, and trains went by all day. We heard them in the early summer mornings booming away shrouded in the mist that came right up to Grandmother's box hedge. When it spun up into the sky above the fir trees there they were, train after train of waving khaki figures.

Sometimes there were cattle trains grinding slowly up to Guildford, and I waved to them too. My mother must have seen the grim and obvious irony of this, because it was 1916 and the expectation of life of a boy sent to the

Somme battle was often not much more than a couple of weeks.

At night the owls hunted under the moon across the mysterious meadows and plantations. The wind whispered in the ivy, and a spider spun up to the ceiling looking big and black in the candle flame. Downstairs low voices went on talking, and talking, for Uncle Bill, Mother's younger brother, was back from the front. He smelled of uniform and tobacco. He used to rub his bristly face against mine and throw me up to the parlour ceiling.

At last they would come upstairs. Beds would creak and the air fill with the reek of extinguished candles. Then I would lie and listen for a sound that never failed all that summer: the sound of men marching through the night.

It would begin very faintly at first as the night wind strengthened, then get louder and louder until you could hear the chink of chains against limber wheels, and the sharp hoof-beats of officers' horses as they rode up and down the column calling out orders.

Sometimes there was singing, and a great roaring negative to the question 'Are we downhearted?' called out bravely to the night in the accents of a county few would see again.

I remember the laughter, and the sound of striking matches, and how the steady tramp of feet would die away until it was no more noticeable than the kitchen clock. Then I would fall asleep and wake at dawn to look out between wet ivy leaves to see another column going by in the early sunlight that glinted on brass and silver and saddle leather.

Cocks crew and the milkman came lugging his heavy bucket. The postman clicked the gate and stood watching, drinking the cup of tea Grandmother always gave him. Still they passed, their boots white with Surrey dust that would soon be Flanders clay, thousands of young men off to the battle of the Somme.

For a few weeks our country lives kept in step with the march of history. Then the leaves began to fall from the chestnut tree and we took the conkers to the village school in linen bags—to be crushed for oil I think. The garden smelled of spilt roses and autumn, and the road was empty except for transport pulled by delicate-limbed mules that never stopped twitching their long ears.

The battle was over, and Uncle Bill had left his foot in no-man's-land and we went back to Tyneside for the rest of the war. On the way we broke our journey in London to visit my other grandfather. I had never seen him before, but I was familiar with his portrait which dominated our kitchen wall. This was more difficult than it sounds because there were fourteen pictures altogether. He had to compete with 'Highland Cattle', 'Nymphs Surprised While Bathing', several wedding groups, and a huge inky-black oil painting called 'The Stabled Stallion'.

I used to lie on the sofa when I was convalescent after measles and study each picture in turn, but I always came back to this bearded man with his dark mane of hair, arrogant eyes, and sarcastically smiling lips. He hung high above an innocuous print of 'Hay-making in Hampshire'. This was mostly because my mother didn't like him—he wasn't her father—and for a long time my curiosity about him remained totally unsatisfied. Mother would talk all day about *her* father, but 'Ask your father!' was her tart reply to any question about my paternal ancestor.

I did ask my father, but somehow he always seemed

to be going to work or coming back from it, or asleep in the back bedroom and liable to be cross if disturbed for frivolous reasons. Sometimes I hardly saw him for days, but standing at our front door you could see a piece of the river and a half-built warship and Father's little box travelling along its swinging cables so it seemed possible to keep in touch with him.

He hadn't always been a crane-driver, Mother said. He'd fought in the Boer War and been a groom, a prisoner warder, a park-keeper, and several other things. She said he was too proud to stick at anything long—'Just like the old man,' she nodded sharply at the portrait, and it grinned sardonically back at her. 'Never got over being educated above his station.' Mother had left the village school at twelve.

'What *was* Grandfather?' I asked my father one night as he buckled on his shiny black belt and picked up his bait in the spotted red handkerchief.

'A lawyer,' he answered, smiling like his father in the picture, and off he went to lift steel plates for the shell of a new destroyer. A lawyer! Young as I was, I knew that lawyers were a cut above crane drivers. Surely Mother should have been proud of him. But she wasn't. She scowled at his picture, and I noticed she always gave it a quick glance if the word 'prison' was mentioned. I knew lawyers sent people to prison, but Mother's look almost implied that Grandfather had been connected with prison in a much less respectable capacity. I was very nearly right. Hardly had Grandfather qualified in his profession than he had had to flee to America to avoid a debtors' prison.

It was like Mr. Micawber. When I read Dickens later I

imagined him dodging his creditors down lanes and alleys till he reached Liverpool docks to stow away on some great Yankee clipper. Perhaps it wasn't as dramatic as that, but something of the sort certainly happened.

Just over a hundred years ago the Civil War was raging when he reached America, and with his usual recklessness Grandfather joined the army of the north and campaigned with Abraham Lincoln's troops for the next few years. Then he came home—probably for the same reason that he set out, my mother observed grimly.

He settled in London, patented a little invention—no one seemed to know quite what—and founded his family: a daughter who went on the variety stage, and four sons who all ran away and fought in South Africa while their father, as belligerent and imprudent as ever, was a pro-Boer whose windows were broken by angry Londoners time and again.

I found this out bit by bit, and Grandfather grew to be a kind of hero to me, much to Mother's disgust.

'Where is Grandfather buried?' I asked once in sentimental tones, thinking I would make a pilgrimage to his grave when I was older.

'Buried!' she exclaimed. 'He isn't even dead. Lives on his own in London.'

That was why we were going to see him on our way back to Tyneside. I remember the day. It must have been early autumn. The streets seemed full of limping soldiers in hospital blue. Our cab clattered over Waterloo Bridge to some dingy street of high Victorian houses north of the river. An old woman sweeping up torrents of leaves with a besom directed us to Grandfather's room.

It was an attic at the top of the house. The floor was

bare and dust grated under our feet like sand. There was a sofa, a table, a chair and a big battered trunk. On the wall were some faded photographs, one of a girl in soubrette costume looking roguish—my Aunt Terry. The mantelpiece was littered with old clay pipes and unpaid bills. My hero lay on the sofa. He seemed very very old. His beard was white like Father Christmas's and his eyes were wet like those of an old spaniel. Mother sat on the one chair and talked primly about the family. In time he livened up and began to look more like his portrait. I roamed about the big almost empty room, and looked out over a sea of grey roofs through more smoke than there must have been at Gettysberg, to the river, and St. Paul's cross swimming in the clean air above it. Very softly I opened the trunk. There was Grandfather's uniform and his big cavalry sword.

Suddenly the old man was beside me. His knotted hands drew out a forage cap. He put it on, and immediately became an old Yankee general. He took out the sword, uncleaned since his demobilisation I should think, and whirled it about like Excalibur.

'On to Richmond!' he shouted in a high nasal voice.

Excalibur stuck in the lintel above the door, and when he had plucked it out we had to help him back to the sofa. He lay down trembling and I tried on his blue cap which had fallen on the floor. It felt limp and lifeless.

'Did you ever get to Richmond, Grandfather?' I asked presently, but the sword-play had exhausted him and he was asleep. Mother removed a bottle of pleasant-smelling straw-coloured liquid from under his cushion, went to the window and emptied it over north London. She meant well, I suppose, and certainly drink was still a curse in

1916. We left some money under his tobacco jar and crept out without wakening him.

My grandfather died soon after the war, and his landlady sold off his few odds and ends. There was money owing, of course. Father was angry, but the slump had begun and he was unemployed by then. I grieved for the uniform and the sword, but they are irretrievably lost. Those limp blue garments Grandfather once wore so proudly will have been given to the ragman many years ago now.

Perhaps the sword survives somewhere. I like to think of a boy, romantic as I was then, fingering that old sabre, and wondering which war it was used in: never guessing that it once crossed the elegant blades of those gentlemen of the south that Grandfather fought when he was a mercenary soldier a hundred years ago.

Back on Tyneside, only three miles from the coast, we felt exposed to attack. When I played in the summers of 1917 and 1918 on South Shields beach and looked out over the grey North Sea I used to be afraid because there was only this desolate stretch of water between me and the Kaiser.

'Somewhere out there,' my mother would say, guessing my cowardly thoughts, 'the Navy is protecting us.' But I couldn't see it—a tribute perhaps to the new art of camouflage. What I could see were the occasional Zeppelins lying low on the skyline. They were waiting for nightfall to come up the Tyne and bomb the steelworks. When we saw them we'd get the tram home quickly as if it would be safe there.

Sure enough, that night a destroyer would come screaming up the river. The gas would flicker and go out. Then my mother would light a little oil lamp that made our bedroom like Grandmother's in far-off safe Surrey, and stand a writing case round it to stop any light leaking out between the edge of the window and the dark green paper blind to guide the Kaiser to Father's crane.

Some people ran out into the fields beyond the town, but we never did. Mother would sit knitting socks and Balaclavas like everyone did then, and saying her prayers while anti-aircraft guns shook the house, and the Zepps dropped their primitive missiles along the river line.

At school the war was always with us. It was reflected in our dress—sailor blouses and navy coats with brass buttons, and admirals caps, stiff with gold braid. They had little inset pictures of Beatty and Jellicoe on them. We sang war songs every day with cheerful unconcern, especially when it got near to four o'clock and there didn't seem much else to do. 'A long long trail' could make me cry even then, and the dusk which blurred the outline of the blackboard and made us dim and mysterious to one another was full of excitement and emotion. We collected badges which we brightened with Meppo on a Friday when the fire-irons got their weekly clean. I wore the silver running horse of Hanover because father had been in the West Yorks.

Most of our teachers were women then. Ours was a bad-tempered old lady who drank whisky behind the blackboard and used to thump me because I couldn't make a letter 'f'. She stood me in a corner once and made me admit I was a 'daft German sausage'. Everything German was bad. We passed a house on our way home where Germans were said to live, and never failed to shout insults at its dirty windows. Sometimes a mild bewildered face appeared between the ragged lace curtains. Years later we found that a Scots recluse had lived there.

The few Germans in our town were pork butchers, and they had a bad time. Their windows were constanly being broken, especially if a ship had gone down or an attack failed. Only the fighting men, who sometimes came to tea and gave me pennies and miniature silk flags out of their cigarette packets (my mother used to decorate cushion covers with them), astonished us by speaking of the enemy in almost friendly terms. But mostly they never mentioned the war at all.

One day we went to tea at a barracks at Tynemouth. Out on the square the soldiers sat in shirt-sleeves at long tables drinking tea out of basins. I fell over one asleep on the floor. He was fully dressed with his rifle beside him. I suppose he'd just come off guard duty. I felt very guilty, but he only grinned and winked and settled down again on his hard bed. We had kippers for tea in the serjeants' mess and my Uncle Leo, just back from Malta, poured brown beer into glasses and sang 'Speak to me, Thora'. I'd never seen my father so happy.

On the way home we saw searchlights sweeping the sea, and heard the roar of shipyards and shell factories, that, like the guns in France, never ceased throughout the war.

The end came one grey windy Monday. I got out of bed and pulled up the fraying paper blind we'd used all through the war. There was a November sky, pale as a plate.

The wind blew the smoke from the houses opposite level like a lancer's pennon. North-west it came from, where the Roman Wall was and the moors and Hexham Abbey. They were always telling us about these things at school but I'd never seen them yet. Only the broad green lower Tyne smelling of sewage, and rusty iron, and raw paint from the shipyards. Only a long wall with jagged glass on top, above which masts and funnels glided by on their way to the sea.

The last door banged, and iron-shod feet ran down Grenville Street. Half past seven the brass alarm clock said, and a pit buzzer whined to prove it. You could hear an intermittent rumbling like distant gun-fire. That was my mother and her neighbours rolling out their poss-tubs. It was washing day.

I ought to have been getting ready for school, but the influenza that was to kill more people than the war had begun, and it was closed. My father was on the six-to-two shift. I sat down to dress on the empty chair where he kept his work clothes. It smelled of him, and of oil. In the kitchen I heard my mother stirring porridge and frying me a piece of dark brown wartime bread in Father's bacon fat. Sometimes he left a little bit of lean for me. While I ate it, Mother banged away at the copper fire. It roared gloriously and then went out. Mother split some tough oven wood on the stone floor of the kitchen and tried again. There was a resinous smell, smoky spluttering, and then silence.

She appeared at the kitchen door, pushing back white wispy hair with a black hand.

'It won't draw, son,' she said despairingly. 'The wind must be the wrong way.'

It often was. Sometimes the fire took hours to get going. Then the iron door would glow red and the copper lid jump madly up and down emitting puffs of scalding steam.

We lived in the upstairs flat, and Mother carried all the boiling water down to the yard in a two-handed bath. She filled the poss-tub, then boiled the clothes in another copper full of water and carried them down too.

'Can't we wash on Tuesday, Mother?' I asked, but I knew we never could.

Mrs. Hanlon from downstairs left off possing her clothes and came to inspect the fire. She was panting and reaked of blue-mottle soap. Her eyes roved round to the teapot. Possing is hard work. Mother mutely poured her a cup. It had been standing on the hob since six-thirty and you could trot a mouse on it, as she observed appreciatively.

The kitchen was filling with acrid blue smoke.

'Ye've got a stoppage in that ould chimney, Mrs. Barton dear,' she said. 'Send your bairn to Tweddle's for a pennorth of gunpowder. That'll shift it. Begob, it's shifted a lot these four years.'

She laughed shortly and thumped down our carpetless back stairs. Her husband had been in minesweepers.

I took a penny and ran to the chemist's hopping over the drying semi-circles of pavement outside each door.

'Gunpowder, hinney?' asked old Mr. Tweddle, peering from behind his vast bottles of lovely red and blue liquids. He looked at a big clock on the wall. 'You'd better hurry up, son, there's not much time left.'

I wondered what he meant. It was only a quarter to eleven. 'We've all day,' I thought. 'Perhaps he means it'll rain, but it won't. There's too much wind.'

Our back lane was full of sheets billowing like galleon sails and Geordie Rutherford, the coalman, was holding back his restive black horse and shouting, 'Howway, girls, lift your clothes up for us!' They shrieked at his ribaldry, and looped their bedclothes high and clear of his grimy sacks.

On wet days when he was in a bad mood he often drove straight through and the angry women followed him shaking their fists like a Greek chorus. We never hung our clothes in the lane. It was more genteel to dry them in your backyard, and what was more, you concealed your deficiencies that way.

Mother wrapped the gunpowder tightly in a couple of copies of *Home Chat* and advanced on the copper like a Grenadier. She opened the door where a tiny flame still licked the charred wood. In went the innocuous-looking paper wad; slam went the oven door. We held it shut with the yard broom and waited.

There was a curious silence for a few moments. Our canary, whose cage hung on a rusty nail outside the window, stopped trilling. The washing women in the lane were listening for something. Very faintly in the wind we could hear a church bell.

Then there was a crash that sent us both back against the kitchen door, a vibration up my arms I was to remember twenty-five years later when I first fired a rifle, an exciting smell of destruction, and away went the copper fire so fast we couldn't shovel fuel in quickly enough.

As if our small explosion had been some sort of ceremonial signal, all the buzzers and hooters on the river Tyne started up. Bells rang. The ragman trumpeted. A seaplane from the North Sea, three miles away, swept low over the town.

When the uproar died down there was cheering in the street and from far away men's voices singing the saddest of war songs. It had been a long long trail indeed. My mother's tears rolled down into the washtub.

'What is it, Mother,' I asked anxiously, 'is the Kaiser coming?'

She hugged me with a warm soapy arm.

'It's over!' she sobbed again and again. 'It's all over!'

I opened the copper door and smelled cordite and felt—disappointed I suppose—while the wind in the yard outside made a noise like guns and my mother went on quietly crying for the lost generation.

At school a week or two later a man came round the classrooms. We had just been promoted to ink and I looked up from my spattered copy book where I'd been struggling with 'Speech is silver; silence is golden,' and wiped my dripping fingers on my sailor blouse as he came in. He wore a red cloak and carried a cocked hat just like Nelson's. Round his neck was a long gold chain.

I don't remember what he said—I hardly ever listened to or understood grown-ups in those days, but it sounded vaguely apologetic. Then he disappeared between two important-looking men in black and we heard him being driven away in a carriage.

'The Kaiser!' whispered Charlie Simms, but whether he spoke in jest or earnest I never knew. I accepted the fact without question. Nor did it dawn on me for many years that the dreaded German monarch reputed to be in exile in Holland would scarcely have been so immediately available. But eventually I saw a mayor in his ceremonial dress and realised my error.

The war went on dominating minds and hearts right through our youth. The myth grew rather than faded. Kitchener on the tattered poster at the end of our street might disappear—drowned again in cold northern rain—

but at school we began to be taught by haggard young men who roared into the playground on Indian motor cycles and made us drill like guardsmen.

Certainly it was dimmed a little when ordinary threadbare fellows knocked at the door with writing paper and boot-laces. They had an empty sleeve or a cork leg like Uncle Bill, and from their lapels hung the famous Mons Star. It began to die in the twenties when the Last Post ceased to thrill us, and the silence wasn't quite so silent.

There were marching feet to be heard again, but they only crossed the market square, broke step, and shuffled upstairs into the labour exchange.

And in the literary world which I kept in touch with through the reviews strewn on the green tables of the Mechanics' Institute, a young German with an arresting face detonated an explosion with a book about how quiet it had been on the Western Front.

A Band in the Park

THE first thing I heard on a Sunday morning was the single bell of St. Margaret's a few streets away ringing for early service, and the next the soft thud of my mother closing the front door as she went out to it alone.

From the other bedroom I could hear my father snoring gently. Outside there was the light clatter of a milk-cart, and presently the paper boy's cry—a little muted in honour of the day.

When I went to the door in hastily donned shirt and trousers to buy the *Herald* and *Pictorial* the street was deserted. There were no overalled figures hurrying to work with their blue cans and wicker baskets of bait, no steel-shod pitmen, jet-black from the shift, no knockers-up in men's peaked caps and close-hugged shawls shuffling home to a welcome cup of tea. My father's crane, with its little box in which he travelled to and fro all the week, stood motionless against the blue sky, and shipyards and steelworks lay oddly silent in the summer sunlight except for an occasional short roar of steam, or the hollow clang of falling metal. I used to think the whole river front slept on Sundays, like a great beast worn out with the exertions of the week.

On the chair in our kitchen, Father's work clothes hung limp and greasy, smelling of oil and rust and 'the works'. I searched in his pockets and found an old bacon sandwich. It was dry and warped, but eaten in bed it kept me going until I woke again an hour later.

Mother would be back then, singing 'Praise to the holiest' in her soft Sussex voice as she fried the breakfast. Down in the yard Father cleaned our shoes and his best boots. Everything smelled fresh and clean. We'd all been bathed the night before in the tin bath that hung, still dripping slightly, on a nail in the scullery. Pan after pan of boiling water had been needed to fill it. Mother was always tired after Saturday's shopping and cleaning and bathing, but with Sunday dinner and the baking she wasn't going to get much rest today either. It was different for boys and men. By midmorning Father and I were dressed in our best, and while Mother rammed logs under the temperamental oven off we went—he to his allotment and I to church. He didn't work on the allotment on a Sunday, of course. He might pick a bunch of flowers, of lift a lettuce, but mostly the men in their best blue suits only gossiped and looked critically at their own and one another's leeks.

No one played in the streets on a Sunday then. If you had best clothes you came out to walk or worship. If you hadn't you stayed in until Monday. It became a cruel custom in a town where many were poor during the slump, and I am very glad to see that there is little or no dressing up on Sundays today, and no need any more to be immured every seventh day for lack of a best suit and different shoes.

Until my father was out of work, however, I was one

of the élite who could walk abroad and appear in church. We went three times a day, and though it could be boring, church was no worse than school or home, and just as comfortably familiar. The Book of Common Prayer and the Authorised Version gave a lining to the minds, and a turn of phrase to the speech, of even the least literate of us.

Most children went to some sort of church. For one thing there wasn't much else to do except walk. Toys and games were forbidden both inside and out. You couldn't even run on a Sunday.

This should have been terribly restricting to energetic children, but I don't remember that it was. There was an exhilaration in being differently dressed and seeing the girls in their finery—muffs in winter and white gloves in summer. Everyone wore buttonholes then, and on Sundays we smelled of sweet peas and pansies and lavender water and the scented sweets we often bought to suck through a long sermon. At midday the streets were still quiet except for an occasional green-trumpeted gramophone pouring out Foster Richardson or Madame Clara Butt through an open front window. The odours of roast beef and Yorkshire pudding drifted deliciously all over town, and in every oven a rice pudding gently bubbled and browned.

This gave rise to a peculiar piece of class distinction. The lower orders who had lain in bed too long found that they had only time for the first course of Sunday dinner before Sunday school, and went back for pudding afterwards.

I well remember a new girl-friend tentatively exploring my background and at last asking boldly, 'Do yous get your rice before Sunday school or after?' and her relief that I belonged to the acceptable people who had all their dinner at the same time.

After Sunday school somebody's Prize Silver Band played in the park—of which much more hereafter—and made an exciting background for our early amorous adventures. These never seemed to get far—a smile, a wink, or from the real Don Juans the daring 'Canny leg hinney!' and an outraged shove into the geraniums while the cornet-player filled the languid teatime air with 'Alice, where art thou?' to which the ritual answer was for some reason: 'Under the bedclothes'. I liked Sunday tea. Mother wore her white blouse and gold chain. She presided, a little pale but triumphant, over girdle scones, jam tarts, and three sorts of cake. Father didn't pour his tea into the saucer to cool, or leave his jacket off, and of course I wasn't allowed to read.

The church bells began at six o'clock. I remember them best in the early autumn when the yellow gas lamps were lighted and the wind blew seagulls about September skies. Father brushed his bowler and Mother sorted out prayer books and gave me a clean scented handkerchief.

There was often exaltation at evensong when the choir sang 'Take up thy cross, the Saviour said', and the wind muttered gruffly in the handful of trees outside, and Elizabeth, whose father was a doctor, knelt by a pillar in the gathering gloom, lovely and remote as an angel.

I sometimes frightened myself with 'Day of wrath O day of mourning' during the sermon, and thought sadly that for my sins I should soon be with the 'ruined men and angels', but the sharp walk home through the chilly sea-winded streets cheered me up again, and there was always cold meat and mint sauce and delicious little scallops of fried potato for supper.

The gas hissed reassuringly as I read Jack London and Father looked to his work clothes, and wound the brass alarm clock up for morning. And from the river a ship hooted a deep warning as she moved up to Newcastle through the October mist.

Early to bed then, listening to Mother laying the breakfast things, and once my Sunday clothes were off and my jersey and shorts laid out for the morning, my thoughts turned, not unwillingly, to school and play.

When I woke I heard doors being clashed, and buzzers blowing, and the *North Mail* being cried by barefoot stentors, and I couldn't help being a little bit glad it was Monday again, and that a whole week separated me from the solemnities of another Sunday.

The highlight of Sunday for me, and indeed for most people, was the band in the park. We heard it strike up at three o'clock just before Sunday school ended, and the jolly strains of the opening march—'Colonel Bogey' or 'With sword and lance'—contrasted excitingly with Miss Hammond's lugubrious playing of 'Now the day is over,' and our feeble uninterested singing. Sometimes we were halfway up the aisle after a scarcely attempted 'Amen' when the curate raised his hand in hurried blessing, and transfixed us for a moment in various attitudes of escape.

Then we raced up Park View, through the big iron gates, past the sloping lawns where Little Doritt and lobelia spelled out 'R. Anderson, Mayor, 1925', and across the green to see silver instruments flashing in the sun against a background of scarlet and pipeclay splendour. All the decent part of the town was situated near the park, and most of its more respectable citizens were perched round the bandstand on green metal seats giving attentive ears to *Zampa* and *Aïda*.

On the grass, however, a raffish element from that other town beyond the railway, that town of shipyards, steel-works, and blast-furnaces, lay coupled in oblivious ecstasy. And between the solid matrons and bowler-hatted fathers, and these lovers, who, horizontal and anonymous, were no more than convenient obstacles, we ran and leaped and shouted, drunk with freedom and fresh air and the heady euphoria induced by sounding brass, entirely forgetting, temporarily at least, the decorum due to the day.

I didn't know where the bands came from until Fred told me. No one in Grenville Street played anything but the piano, and I thought of them all as soldiers, these splendidly clad musicians. When they marched away at last down Park Road, and left the drab dispersing crowd and overturned chairs and empty bandstand, I imagined them to be bound for some ultimate corner of a foreign field.

'Gerraway, Barty,' said Fred, 'they're mostly pitmen like me granda, and the farest they'll get's the Engineers' Arms.'

There was one exception, however, to Fred's sweeping generalisation, the Scottish Pipe Band. They came only once a summer—all the way from the Highlands, I claimed vehemently. The glamour of the '45 and Bonnie Prince Charlie, and the more recent fierce fighting in Flanders, surrounded them.

From the moment the drums began to beat, and the pipes gave their curious preliminary wail, I was completely lost. Not for me on that Sunday the chase round flower-beds and over somnolent lovers. I stood by the rail that separated us from those brawny bonneted giants, an invisible claymore in my hot hand, and my eyes full of tears as 'Lochaber no more' mourned across the park. To my astonishment Fred didn't care much for the pipers. He annoyed me by insisting that all their tunes, though differently named on the programme, were really the same.

'Here we go again, Barty,' he would sigh with weary resignation, and indeed, though I wouldn't have admitted it for worlds, perhaps there was something even to my besotted ears in what he said.

'Ye want to come and listen to me granda's band next Sunday,' he boasted. 'None of this 'nya, 'nya stuff. When they play "1812" ye know it isn't "Hearts and Flowers".'

Fred's grandfather was the solo cornet-player in the Lawton Colliery Prize Silver Band. An old man, his touch was still true, but his higher notes tended to falter now and then, and it was known that several younger musicians coveted his place. But none of them would have dreamed of accelerating his retirement by drowning him. That, however, was what almost happened one Saturday afternoon in the summer of 1925.

Of course, this Sunday ration of music, important though it was to us, wasn't quite all we ever got, though we were far in those days from the time when any kind of music would be available at almost any moment. Our regular diet at home and school was pretty meagre.

We were too poor to have acquired a piano in the affluent days of the Great War. My father sometimes unbuckled his greasy belt after tea, and sitting back in the armchair picked out 'Robin Adair' or the march of his old regiment on the flute, and sometimes he sang things like 'Anchored' and 'My Old Shako' at local concerts.

My mother had a wide repertoire of hymns, and when especially happy (which alas was seldom in her later years) sang a music-hall song of the nineties that began, 'Strolling one day through the Lowther Arcade, a place for children's toys.'

It must have reminded her of far-off days when she was a housemaid in Sloane Square, slipping out to post a letter to my father, then a West Yorks sergeant sweating across the veldt to Colenso with Buller and young Winston Churchill.

There wasn't much music in Fred's house either. His father rocked the current baby to 'Geordie haud the bairn' and other esoteric Tyneside songs, and we were sometimes made to listen to extracts from oratorio for which he had a passion. This existed oddly but amiably with his two other interests, atheism and the rising Labour Party, and it was not unusual to see him moved to tears by 'I know that my Redeemer liveth', issuing with more power than sweetness from the distorting trumpet of the gramophones of forty years ago.

At school we thought of music as a subject and rated it accordingly; not to be feared like arithmetic, nor given over to daydreaming like history or geography, but just a bore. You had to sing, graduating from the hated modulator and misinterpreted hand signals to something called 'staff or stave', where we were taught to memorise the lines (what for I wonder?) by the amusing mnemonic 'Eat Good Bread Dear Father'.

Other classes always seemed to have more attractive songs. Standard IV, I remember, sang a lovely one about

Tynemouth Abbey—or did I just think it lovely because their music lesson was on a Friday afternoon when we were idling away our time with silent reading and the endless bliss of the weekend lay ahead? The sun slanted in through the steamed-up window across my copy of *Lorna Doone* (I'd failed as usual to get *Sabre and Spurs—a tale of the Light Dragoons*) and their voices rising and falling in sweet melancholy sent me off into rapturous fancies—broken now and then by the unmistakable sound of someone being caned.

'We might go to Tynemouth Abbey tomorrow,' I said to Fred after school. We'd often seen its ruined walls rising in grey and ancient dignity above the cliffs on the Northumberland side of the Tyne estuary when we'd been plodging at Shields, but had never been closer than that.

'Not tomorrow,' objected Fred. 'Me granda's coming to stay the night and I've got to stop in for him while me ma's down the street.'

I recalled that this was the Sunday his grandfather was playing in the park, and wondered if I would see the old musician.

'Come round, Barty,' said Fred hospitably. 'Me da's going to a union meeting and we'll be on wor own.'

I was under a temporary ban from Fred's house at that time. A week or two before I'd climbed up to see the time on the face of their small and disfigured clock. Unfortunately, I'd steadied myself by holding on to the edge of the mantelpiece. To my horror, and too late, I'd found it not to be firm like ours, but just a loose plank laid across two brackets. The subsequent crash brought half the neighbours in. 'I thought the French had landed!' exclaimed old Mrs. Gill, who looked ancient enough to have remembered when they were expected. But lying amongst the broken ornaments and old bills and letters and bits of the now defunct clock and gallons of flower-water, I found it hard to join in their amusement. So later did Fred's father and mother; hence the ban.

On Saturday we all went our messages—to the depot for our week's supply of coal—always trundled home in a steel-shod barrow—and later to the shops for bread.

I was a bit late because Doris was at the coal depot. She was wheeling her barrow away from the scales as I pushed mine under, and while Black Jack filled it up, I nerved myself to say, 'Are ye coming to the park tomorrow? Fred Gray's granda's playing a cornet solo.'

She opened her blue eyes wide and tossed her newly bobbed hair. 'He's a bit old for me,' she said, but her look implied that perhaps I wasn't.

'Howway, son,' broke in Black Jack irritably. 'I've more to do than wait for you to stop sloppin' on with yer tart.'

Doris fled with a high colour that I hoped wasn't anger, and I raced my load home. Fred was ahead of me, his white calico pillow-case full of bread.

'Two o'clock, Barty,' he cautioned, his mouth crammed with warm black top crust.

If only I hadn't had to go for bread, too, nothing untoward would have happened to Fred's grandfather. I was late and took a short cut across the brickfield. It wasn't really a brickfield, though we always called it that, but a devastated area near a disused pitshaft. There were bricks—thousands of them—and sometimes we built forts and had battles with the boys from Nelson Street. There was a pond too, a noisome stretch of water, the foreshore of which was covered with the unsavoury remains of drowned animals. Acrid smoke, forced up through the slaty soil and coarse grass from subterranean fires, made the place reek of sulphur and when Mr. Peacock described the destruction of Sodom and Gommorah in a scripture lesson Fred whispered to me, 'Just like wor brickfield!'

I usually gave it a wide berth, being afraid of the Nelson Street boys, but I took a chance this Saturday morning, as the place seemed deserted. I was wrong. Before I was half-way across the burning marl three of them descended on me with wild cries. They had short appropriate first names like Twit and Pratt. It was my string bag they were after. Pratt held me while Twit took it, and the third, a small ginger boy thought to be mad, turned out the loaves and substituted the lifeless body of a once handsome black cat.

Then, after twisting my wrist once or twice, more as a matter of routine than with any real hostility, they made off to their redoubt in which blazed a small sacrificial fire. I picked up the bread, lucky really to have it, and made my way home.

However, in the afternoon, as I cautiously approached Fred's back door, I saw them again. It turned out later that they were only looking for me to give the string bag back, but such was my unhappy experience of Nelson Street boys that I fled as soon as I saw them. This was too great a temptation, and they gave immediate and delighted chase. Luckily Fred's back door wasn't bolted, and I was able to slip in before they overtook me.

'Nelson Streeters!' I gasped as I slammed the door. Fred rammed the bolts home, and resourcefully dragged his mother's heavy mangle across the doorway as an additional barricade.

Soon large stones began to pound the door and to be lobbed over like mortar-fire into the backyard. We retreated into the shelter of the hen cree and considered tactics.

Our only missiles seemed to be these stones and they wouldn't last long. At the same moment we both noticed the small water-butt, and looked at each other in a wild surmise. Could it be got to the top of the brick parapet over the back gate, and its contents poured down on the invaders like boiling lead from a besieged castle? Fred's eye lit up. He did not think of his mother's loss of her summer store of 'soft' water for baths and her washing. Quickly we brought out the big kitchen table, cut down the clothes-line, and chivvied the hens back into their cree.

By making use of some convenient iron rings in the wall we raised the small tub up on to the table, then got its rim level with the top of the wall. The stone-throwing had stopped momentarily, and we could hear nothing from below. No doubt Twit and Pratt and the third man—Cunny, I remember he was called—were plotting their next move directly below us.

'Heave-ho, Barty!' gasped Fred, and we grasped the wet mossy base of the tub and heaved.

Up it went. Then as the water poured out in an immense dirty cascade on whoever lurked beneath, the suddenly lightened barrel slipped from our excited fingers and disappeared. We heard it fall on the cobbles with a hollow clang. We also heard a gasp and an unearthly cry.

Cautiously we raised our heads above the level of the wall, and looked down. There was the empty barrel still rolling gently in the gutter. There were our enemies, just across the lane and disappointingly bone-dry. Unusual expressions of alarm almost made their faces unrecognisable, and following the direction of their horrified stares we heaved ourselves up a bit farther and looked directly downwards. On the drenched cobbles, and gasping like a hooked fish, lay a small scarlet-clad old gentleman. In one feebly agitating hand he still held a shiny black case—which had burst open to show the silver splendour of his beloved cornet.

From all directions housewives and shirt-sleeved men, disturbed at their Saturday-afternoon tasks, were hurrying to the rescue.

'It's me grandfather!' gasped Fred.

I couldn't speak. Neither could he again. Silently we put the table in the kitchen, and slipped the doorbolts quietly back. But when someone opened it and an anxious procession bore the unconscious old musician indoors to apply artificial respiration Fred and I were halfway to South Shields.

For an hour or so we hung about the quaysides there, trying to pluck up courage to stow away on a Danish butter boat, or the *Highlander*, in with her cargo of whisky, but in the early summer dark we had to drift slowly back to our separate destinies.

Mine included the whole of Sunday immured in my bedroom, where I read bound volumes of *The Quiver* (1895), full of stories of curates in Norfolk jackets in love with penniless governesses. Late in the afternoon I opened my window cautiously and listened. The breeze was in the right direction, the park less than a mile away. Perhaps Doris was there, resplendent in London Tan or whatever the colour was that year, impatiently waiting for me to arrive with the St. Stephen's contingent. I imagined her foot tapping with unmusical boredom while the Lawton Colliery Prize Silver Band burst into 'Poet and Peasant', but I was too miserable to care much. I still felt like a murderer.

When the time came for the cornet solo it wasn't left out. Someone played it of course—played it jolly well, too—though such easy skill seemed a little callous when Fred's grandfather lay somewhere between life and death.

I was so preoccupied with those gloomy speculations that it was some time before I heard frantic whistling from below.

At last I looked out. There was Fred, chastened indeed, but actually smiling.

'Did ye hear him, Barty?' he shouted in a kind of whisper. 'The game old beggar! Me da told him it was likely to be his bloody swan-song, but it was no use telling him. He would go.'

As a matter of fact, it wasn't his last appearance, but whether his subsequent and long-overdue honourable retirement was hastened at all by our exploit, who can say?

It all seems such a long time ago now, but every time I hear the strains of a cornet solo drifting across the sunburnt greens and regimented flower-beds on a summer afternoon I remember that dreadful weekend, and the Sunday when for once I missed the band in the park.

A Few Public-school Men

As the bus streamed steadily south through the bright sunlight of that early spring morning when I left Tyneside to seek my fortune in London, Durham soon gave place to Yorkshire and that broad county to whatever lies south of it. I wished I had paid more attention to Miss Weston's geography lessons, though the names of the grey stone straggling towns seemed familiar, and as we bumped down their main streets (so-called luxury coaches ran far less smoothly in the early thirties) I thought of the Roman legions who marched north along Ermine Street to their unenviable stint of duty on Hadrian's Wall, and Harold's doomed army hurrying south to London and on to fatal Hastings.

Sometimes I wondered about my case—a cheap and rather frail one made of some substance little better than cardboard—being flung about in the capacious boot of Orange Bros. coach. It contained all that was left of my twenty-odd years in Jarrow except for a few quite worthless pictures and odds and ends put in a linen box and left with a trusted neighbour in her cupboard under the stairs. In my case was a spare suit (Weaver to Wearer, thirty shillings), pyjamas, shaving things, socks, a shirt or two, my favourite books, and, of course, all my poems written out very neatly in a school exercise book.

There must have been forty or fifty of them, all about love and war and unemployment and wanting to die young like Keats. I remember lying half out of bed like the famous picture of Chatterton, and my mother coming in and wondering what on earth I was doing in such an absurd pose.

They weren't good poems, I knew—though I sometimes thought them so—generally early on the morning after I had written them. And I had the word of one of my favourite poets of that time, Edmund Blunden, to confirm this. He thought they were rotten too. I had sent a sheaf of them to him, and I had a letter from him in my wallet, which I had read and re-read until it was nearly in pieces.

Of course, being a gentle poet and also a gentleman, he didn't say my verses were rotten in the direct brutal way of today. But he 'could find no magic word to say about them' and pleaded the frequency of having to read other people's poetry as a factor which might have led him to miss any possible merit in mine, which was very nice of him.

I had written on a piece of quite awful writing paper from a twopenny packet bought at Mrs. Carr's shop at the corner of Grenville Street, and he had, either from tact, absent-mindedness, or mere frugality, answered (in beautiful black script) on the other half of the double page.

It was the first letter I'd ever had from a famous poet, and almost the last, though years later John Betjeman was to be equally kind and almost equally non-committal. But now, as then, I still obstinately think of myself as some sort of failed minor poet rather than anything else.

London, when at last we reached it, did not have any

magic for me at first. I had been there several times before as a small boy on visits to my grandmother, and could remember clopping over Waterloo Bridge in a hansom cab and seeing the (to me) great expanse of gull-haunted Thames and blue-coated wounded soldiers limping along the pavements. My mother was with me and Aunt Rose, a stout lady smelling of camphor who had given me a stiff little white tent for my soldiers.

All my memories of London were of its vastness, and now fifteen or sixteen years later, I thought Trafalgar Square small and shabby, and the river dirty and narrow and not a patch on the dear Tyne at Newcastle. Perhaps I was already beginning to be homesick, but tea at my lodgings—a twelve-mile journey out of London again, somewhere near High Barnet—did something to restore me. They had been found for me by an aunt who was there to welcome me. She was an old lady with hair drawn back from a shrewd kind face, and would have made a good nun if she hadn't belonged to some extreme Protestant sect. I never could quite remember which, but it involved cooking on Saturday so as not to break the Sabbath and walking miles on Sunday because bus- and Tube-drivers ought not to be working.

In spite of this rather forbidding bigotry, she was very kind to me, and in fact to everyone. Later I found she had looked after a crippled woman of no religious faith daily for over thirty years before going to her quite heavy work at a steam laundry in Southgate.

My aunt lived with her widower brother (Aunt Rose's husband) in a tiny cottage full of little jugs from Brighton and Bognor that I was always knocking down, antimacassars and texts. The walls were practically covered with the latter. On the back of the front door it said, cryptically, 'First to the Jews'—Aunt was in some society which hoped to convert them—and even the lavatory—a homely shed down the garden among tall hollyhocks—was not exempt, bearing the inappropriate legend, 'Surely the Lord is in this place,' worked in coloured silks and hung above the toilet paper, a neat stringful of quarter pages from the *Christian Herald*.

She had got me lodgings with a jobbing gardener, a gun-deaf artilleryman with a delightful Oxfordshire accent, a loquacious wife and two small children. There was also a black-browed grown-up son Bill who hardly ever appeared. He would come in from work, rush his tea, and be off again on his racing bike to meet some servant girl up in Holloway. His mother would always wait up for him, and sometimes I awoke at about two o'clock to hear them rowing furiously.

The truth was she was jealous of the girl and suspected (rightly) that Bill was having illicit relations with her. I remember they always prefaced their wildest lies with 'I swear to you if the Lord should take us both tonight . . .' and I'm afraid I often wished he would. There were two other lodgers, a cheerful bricklayer who rode a powerful motor bike, and a stableman from the United Dairies next door—a silent horse-smelling Welshman who seldom spoke and whose English I could never understand a word of.

We communicated by friendly signs, and he once took me up to Hyde Park Corner, where dozens of his fellow exiles, male and female, would congregate and sing 'Cym Rhonda' and other passionately lugubrious Welsh hymns before drifting off usually in pairs across the grass where lovers, in spite of prowling bishops and the chilly spring evenings lay in attitudes of sensual oblivion.

My days, however, were not much more fruitful in High Barnet than they had been at home. There were far fewer men at the labour exchange but the same dearth of jobs. I had no wish to go corn-harvesting in Canada. A friend of mine had been the year before and had come back with tales of overwork, wage-cheating, and sometimes real cruelty. Naturally they didn't want naval architects anywhere at this time. Nor was it as easy as I had thought to get some humble Dickensian clerkship, from which I might rise like a latter-day Dick Whittington. I scanned the lists. I wrote dozens of letters. I wore my precious shoes out seeing the sights and wasted my money on long useless bus journeys.

They seemed only to want pot-barmen, whatever they might be. I imagined it to be something connected with serving drinks or standing long hours over sinks full of dirty glasses, first washing and then polishing them. It seemed unattractive until I remembered that John Masefield had once done it in 'Frisco or New York. What had been good enough for a poet laureate was good enough for me, so I chose a salubrious type of hotel somewhere near Hadley Woods or Cockfosters and reconnoitred it early one morning.

An old bent man was shining up the handles on the big front door like a parody of Gilbert's office boy, with a tin of Meppo and a dirty yellow rag. I ventured closer.

'Is this the place where they want a pot-barman?' I asked.

He stopped polishing, straightened up, and said with a kind of cocky malevolence, ' 'Ook it, chum. I'm 'im.'

Then he bent to his task again and I wandered off across the common to get the bus back to my lodgings and lie on my bed reading 'B' novels from Boots'—early Pamela Hansford Johnson and Margery Sharp—and wondering if I should ever be a writer. Downstairs I often heard Mrs. Tibbs abusing me, and this in spite of my quietness and desperate wish to be of service to her, as 'one of those North Country chaps from where they won't work' (this was a very common attitude in the south at that time), and her husband, whom I liked, defending me in his slow country burr.

This was chiefly because I played with his younger children 'our Daff' and 'our Ron', put them to bed, heard their prayers, and sang them North Country songs. I was not at that time at all fond of young children—most young men aren't—but I was starved of affection and young Ron's frank liking and even Daff's cupboard-love were better than nothing.

Sometimes I hardly spoke to anyone except for formal civilities for days, and this in a city where 'the full tide of human existence' flowed out of Charing Cross and up the Strand to St. Paul's, Fleet Street, and the Tower.

Later I got more ambitious in answering ads. Some offered appointments to 'a few public-school men of the right type to represent a West End business house'. It was the measure of my desperation that I answered these. For, of course, I'm not a public-school man. How could I have been when my father was a crane-driver at our now defunct steelworks? I'd had four years at a grammar school, five as an apprentice naval architect, and several on the dole. Moreover, I was a useless sort of young man, given to writing poetry on the backs of envelopes in tea shops, and falling impossibly in love, but poverty and loneliness were developing a little spirit in me.

I wrote my letter in a firm hand, signified in it my willingness to begin anywhere—right out of sight of the ladder if necessary, and posted it with a feeling of having achieved something.

A day or two later I was on my way to an interview at Peerless House in Baker Street. I wore my neat navy-blue suit—all North Countrymen wore navy blue for best then—and no hat. I still felt vaguely naked without one. Keir Hardie would no doubt have gone to Peerless House in a cap, but I hadn't his confidence. My accent was still imperfectly purged of its North Country vitality and I had no special knowledge of any public schools except Eton, where one of my many aunts had once been a bed-maker.

I needn't have worried. Half an hour later and nine floors up I was sitting with a score of young men even my naive eye could see had never crossed a quad except by accident. The homely accents of Glasgow, Manchester and Stratford-atte-Bowe accepted my equally regional one with a relief as great as my own.

The only possible public-school man present was Major Compton-Hewitt, a gargantuan figure in immaculate sports clothes who stood before us smiling gently and welcoming us to Peerless House in clipped soldierly phrases. He carried over one hairy houndstooth sleeve, as if by some endearing eccentricity, a pair of ladies' silk stockings.

The truth of the situation dawned on some of us immediately, but we sat still, caught like so many rabbits by a genial boa-constrictor. Fascinated, we watched him demonstrate the elegance and desirability of those stockings. Then the complementary virtue of sheer strength.

You could, it seemed, put both fists in the ankle part and stretch it a foot wide without altering the real width one iota. You could rip a sizable pin down the entire length, and the delicate fabric remained unimpaired. Were they silk or highly tensile steel? I wondered. He showed us how to do an 'approach', playing the parts in turn of the salesman and the suspicious housewife. He told us smoking-room stories. At a snap of his fingers, cups of tea appeared. After that it would have seemed churlish not to have signed for our leatherette brief-cases containing a specimen box of three pairs of stockings and an order book. Still in a warm glow, we lighted up his cigarettes, and arranged a rendezvous for the morrow, when a fleet of cars would take us, each with an experienced representative from Peerless House, down to do battle with the Cotswold commuters.

Sheltering from the rain next morning in the porch of the Methodist chapel at High Barnet, it didn't seem such a good idea after all, but I revived a little on the way down. The April showers were soon over.

Parks and gardens flashed by, a more vivid green than I'd ever seen in the north. The almond trees flourished against skies brilliant after sudden storms, and even through the splashed windows and Mr. Joski's cigarette smoke I could feel the charm of the Oxfordshire countryside.

I sat in the front of the little car with Joski, the experienced rep. Behind us were Mr. Katz, and a very unpublic-school man from Bolton named Grindrod. He looked as apprehensive as I felt, and never spoke a word. Joski and Katz chatted to me and I was glad of a little male conversation as a change from the prattle of Daff and Ron and Mrs. Tibbs' endless speculations on the probable sexual behaviour of her elder son. This normal cheerful talk must have gone to my head, because when we were put down in a picture-postcard village I felt ready to sell anything. That feeling didn't last long. When Joski and I fortified ourselves with a pint at the local and the landlord looked contemptuously at our inferior brief-cases I came back to earth with a bump.

I couldn't really see myself selling silk stockings on doorsteps. At home my mother had always closed the front door firmly except to ex-servicemen. To these broken soldiers, with their tarnished medals and pathetic empty sleeves, she gave with a romantic recklessness that cost us many a meal, but to all other travellers she was adamant. However, I was soon following Joski up a white-posted drive to one of those big houses that were set back from the kind of village green that I associated with Farmer George. A man sauntered towards us, tapping highly polished boots with a light crop. I would have fled, but Joski held my arm firmly.

'Don't be servile!' he hissed, as I instinctively cringed and touched my forelock. The man didn't even look at us.

Neither did the frosty maid who answered our tentative ring, but somehow we got to the drawing room, and Joski, fluent irresistible Joski, was demonstrating his wares like an expert conjuror. Out came his notebook and the first box of the day was sold. The stockings were twenty-three shillings for three pairs. One pound went to Peerless House and three shillings into Mr. Joski's pocket. It struck me he'd have to sell a lot of pairs of stockings to go on living.

At the next house the cook was past interest in any

stockings that weren't warm, black and woollen. We were lucky at the third and fourth. At the fifth a great deerhound barred our way, and we retreated backwards as if from royalty.

The sixth and last was a long way back from the road. Expensive gravel glinted in the midday sunshine. From white urns dazzling unknown blue flowers spiralled upwards. A Rolls, immaculate as a Life-Guardsman, stood outside a garage that was bigger than our house in Grenville Street.

Joski lit a cigarette. He smiled. I could feel it coming. 'You do this one,' he said.

I stumbled up the drive feeling every polished pebble through my thin shoes. The hand that I raised to ring the bell trembled. When I was halfway through a gabbled rehearsal of my approach patter the door opened so that I must have seemed to be gibbering. A young woman with an amused eye and the longest cigarette holder I'd ever seen was not in the least disconcerted. She waved me into the morning room, evidently glad of the distraction, and bade me demonstrate.

I muttered as much as I could remember of Compton-Hewett's sales talk. It sounded like a third-rate parody. When I put my dithering fists into the ankle part of the stocking and jerked them outwards, there was a sharp report and a big hole appeared.

I caught my prospective customer's eye and she looked quickly down at the carpet. I tried the pin trick, and the stocking ripped obligingly from top to bottom. It opened out into a ridiculous filmy shape. For a moment I felt like crying. Then my young lady began to laugh. She had an attractive laugh—silvery I suppose, and bubbling, and quite without unkindness. It was infectious. I began to join in. After a few moments we lost control and laughed on and on like people in a gramophone laughing song. I held up the ruined stocking and we began again. Sprawled weakly in elegant armchairs we wept into our handkerchiefs. When I stood up to go I realised that I hadn't laughed like that since I'd left the North Country. It restored something to me. For a minute or two I wondered what it could be. Then it came to me that for the first time in weeks I'd been treated not as a customer, or a nuisance, or a workshy barbarian, but as an ordinary human being. That did me a lot of good, as well as showing me that I couldn't possibly be a door-to-door salesman.

'You done it, boy?' queried Joski, seeing my radiant face as I came down the drive.

'Nothing to it!' I shouted jubilantly, tears of mirth still wet on my cheeks.

He gave me a queer look, and even in the car going back to town he kept saying, 'You all right, boy? Sure you're all right?' though I was great form, singing 'It's a long way to thirty boxes' to the tune of 'Tipperary' with Mr. Katz. Even Mr. Grindrod seemed more at ease, and, though still tongue-tied his smiles almost gave the illusion of speech. At Blackfriars Bridge I wrung Joski's hand and promised to meet him next day on the steps of St. Martin's.

When he'd gone I pitched my brief-case and virgin order book into the Thames.

It was a lovely spring evening. The sky behind Waterloo Station was still deeply blue. A warmish wind knocked the tops off the waves that lapped the foreshore by the Tower.

Along the Embankment, yellow lamps flowered among the spring green like blossoms. I cared nothing now for my threadbare suit and worn-out shoes. I was young. I had met the rich and been treated as a person. The dusk was full of beauty and mystery.

Somewhere, I said to the trees and the sky and the great soaring dome of St. Paul's, somewhere in this astonishing metropolis there must be work worthy of my stature, and tomorrow I would find it!

Football Crazy

DISTURBED rooks caw from lofty elms. There is a babble of voices and a pleasant clinking of cups from the trim marquee. Boundary flags droop in the afternoon heat and so do parents recumbent in deck-chairs along the verge. From time to time a flurry of white figures comes into view and treble voices give tongue as the hopes of their houses tear down the straight. Sports Day—it wasn't at all like that at my elementary school.

To begin with there were no suitable fields for miles and even the park was too far away. No doubt today pupils are conveyed in the ubiquitous coach to where our town stretches its grimy tentacles southwards towards Boldon Hill but schools were not so mobile in the twenties and our sports were held on the tip.

There was nothing green or sylvan about such places—there were several scattered about the town. They were small pieces of spare ground where there used to be a factory for making munitions, or where a row or two of early Industrial Revolution back to back houses had simply fallen down and been abandoned, or even a natural un-filled space left by the formless and unplanned growth of our bricks and mortar wilderness.

They were repositories for tins, old mattresses, prams

and bedsteads, dumps for the sweeps' soot, free storage space for timber baulks and iron pipes belonging to the North Eastern Railway that bisected the town. Some boys dug great holes in them and camped there all the summer holidays. Washing was strung across them each Monday so that they looked like a League of Nations' flag day, but near the middle there was always a hard fairly clear area where football was played for nine months of the year and cricket tolerated for three. On such a tip some summer afternoon our school would hold its annual sports day.

Looked at early in the morning, as Mr. Macdonald saw it when he was deciding whether or not to hold the sports that day, you could even see grass and a dandelion or two around the edge. He would look up at the sun shining through a pale brown perpetual pall of smoke from the riverside works, and with a practised eye decide that it would be a scorcher.

There was no need to mark out the 'field'. Mr. Harris, who had boxed for his battalion of the Northumberland Fusiliers in 1918 and with whom no one would dispute our somewhat shaky right to the tip for the day, would take Standard 7 and spend a pleasant morning clearing away the larger stones, and fixing the only two essential points—a start and a winning post.

Meanwhile all classes chattered over unread Blackies' Model Readers while we were asked who would like to be in what, and were handicapped according to age, and according, in those lean times, to whether or not we possessed a pair of gym shoes.

When school assembled for the afternoon we took off our jackets or jerseys, tucked frocks into knickers (our girls' school joined us on rare occasions like Sports Day), laced our boots tightly, and were ready. Miss Grey's portable gramophone was brought out and placed on a little table in the yard, and to the miniature roar of a Guards band playing 'With Sword and Lance' we marched our fifty yards to the tip which was just behind the drill-hall opposite the school.

Here Mr. Macdonald sat at a trestle table with a huge sheet of paper pinned to a drawing board in front of him. He recorded the winners. Near him on another table were the prizes, guarded by Miss Dean. One would have supposed her forty years of vigilance sufficient, but she was, on my last appearance at my school sports, reinforced by a tall policeman.

This was because of our spectators. Except for a knot of vociferously partisan mothers they were all men. Half our fathers and brothers were already workless in the post-war slump and they formed the bulk of the crowd—divided between interest in the children's chances and silent contempt for all that schools stood for; the shallow classroom idealism that had died long ago in the cut-throat realities of workshop and dole queue.

Young Mr. Jenkins was the judge that year and judging was a job that needed a sharp eye and great firmness. To spot the first three from among the dozen figures that flailed their way down the tip and converged upon poor Mr. Jenkins in a sweaty determined mob took some doing.

I noticed at first that he was grateful to a quiet workman squatting on his hunkers near the winning post who helped him to pick the winners. But in the interval, while the whole school (or at least those lucky ones who had managed to beg a halfpenny) crowded round the Italian's pony cart for ice-cream cornets, I heard Miss Grey tell him that the last four winners were all this man's children. After the interval Mr. Macdonald did the judging himself.

At last it was over; even the staff race which was Mr. Macdonald's annual and ill-advised concession to democracy. Mr. Jenkins retrieved a little of his lost prestige by winning it, but, after all, he was barely twenty and he did try to give the race to Miss Grey, but she tripped over a half-buried chimney pot and was supported from the stricken field.

While the distant gramophone played 'Liebestraume', the vicar of Christ Church distributed the prizes: pocket books, pencils, combs, knives and jewellery that Miss Dean had bought at Piper's Penny Bazaar during the dinner hour.

'Many run,' he murmured ruefully, 'but one receiveth the prize.' His mild Oxford voice effaced for a moment our grimy montage of cranes and condensers. A Tudor lawn sprouted from between the acid cinders. The castellated monstrosity that crowned the drill-hall dissolved into Magdalen Tower.

I noticed Lily Wilson, one of the fleetest girls, being congratulated by her father. She caught my eye and smiled in unaffected pleasure. 'Me da's delighted with us, Barty. He won thirty bob from his mates, and he's given us ten to get a pair of dance shoes. I think I'll get silver.'

Our spectators, bets paid up, sloped off as the gramophone ran down for the fourth time and the prize table was cleared. We formed up and sang 'Be present at our table, Lord,' though many of us would dine alfresco in the street off a hunk of new cake (as we call large flat thin loaves). The fortunate few would get jam on it.

As we dispersed, Lily, who lived in Grenville Street not

far from me, and was still flushed with victory, brought me over a big cornet.

Sports Day, like all annual events, was soon forgotten. Cricket survived in a desultory way through the summer holidays, but with the coming of September football resumed its paramount importance. How could it be otherwise when we lived midway between Newcastle and Sunderland in the great days of wee Hughie Gallagher and Dave Halliday?

We were all football crazy in Grenville Street. They were in Raleigh Street and Drake Court and Hawkins Avenue, too. You'd have expected us to be sea-minded when our streets had names like that, but the sea was three whole miles away, and we seldom got so far, though the east wind sometimes had salt in it and you could hear Souter Point foghorn often on winter evenings.

Even then we played football in the tiny circle of radiance round our lamp, sending young Ronnie out into damp invisibility every few minutes to find the lost ball, while we danced on and off the pavement to keep warm and grimaced at our enormous shadows. Sometimes he found it—a wet bedraggled object picked up in the park by the tennis courts last summer. Sometimes he didn't, and then Bill made him get up early next morning to look for it before the barefoot paper boys who cried the *North Mail* all over our town could find it first.

But football wasn't much fun unless you had a real ball like the one we had at school. Raleigh Street had one, but they were a step higher socially than we were—trimmers and platers lived there—big money men—even one or two clerks who wore bowlers and went to work 'dressed'. Our fathers were overalled to a man; crane-drivers, riveters and labourers, and our pocket money was hardly ever more than the statutory penny. If we had pooled our resources it would have taken the whole season to buy the bladder, never mind the case. Especially as young Ronnie and Sam exhausted their capital long before dinnertime every Saturday and by the time the twelve o'clock buzzer blew were replete with horseshoe turnovers and soda lunches, but penniless for another week.

Rinso Selby (I never knew his real Christian name) called us all together one dry frosty evening, and we sat round the lamp like a pack of jersey-clad nondescript wolves while he told us how the miracle of ball-owning Raleigh Street might be repeated here in humbler Grenville. Rinso was our leader, a tall boy of nearly fourteen. He played for the school team and had once spoken to the famous Charlie Buchan—or so he said, though not many of us believed him. 'There's only one way I can see us getting a ball,' he said, 'and that's to have a bazaar.'

We cheered him to the echo. Bazaars were great. First you got someone to lend you their backyard to have it in, and then you collected things to sell. The girls were always doing it in summer, with cold custard doing duty for ice-cream, and red jelly, and scent cards, and lavender bags, and such like rubbish.

They didn't buy a football, of course—they actually gave the money away to things like the Mayor's Boot Fund for poor 'down the street' sort of children. And no one had ever had one in winter before, but Rinso thought it would be just as easy if we all put our backs into it. The lamplight glinted on his Scout badge and outlined his resolute chin, and we felt momentarily capable of anything.

First we had to find a backyard. 'Lily Wilson's!' shouted Sam. 'She's playing down by yon lamp. I can hear her singing 'Mother, the bells are ringing'.

You could too. The girls played by unspoken agreement at the other lamp unless it was a joint game, and Lily's high sweet voice had just reached 'He's only give her a sixpence and kissed her on the stairs', always a thrilling line to me, when we descended upon her and Winnie and Olive and Gladys and all the ragtail rest with our breathless request.

Lily had left school soon after Sports Day, and her red hair was now piled on top of her head in a grown-up bun. She kept house for her widowed father who drank, and was usually amiable, not caring what she did as long as his pot-pie was ready when he came in from the blast furnaces where he had been lucky enough to find a temporary job.

Some nostalgia for school had made her keep one of her own in her backyard all the summer holiday, and Ritchie Caldwell claimed that she'd done more to teach him to read than Miss Madison and her cane in a whole year in Standard 2.

'You may have it with pleasure next Saturday,' said Lily in her schoolteacher voice that we were all rather afraid of—then, spoiling it a bit, 'Me da'll be in the Golden Fleece till chucking-out time.' Lily's backyard contained an old rain-sodden table from which we could sell things, and a pile of orange boxes waiting to be chopped up for firewood. Rinso's eyes lit up.

'Does yer da want them boxes, Lily?'

She tossed her red head in affectionate contempt.

'He'll never notice they're gone the way he'll be when he comes in, hinneys,' she said.

Rinso's idea was to light a fire in the corner of the yard and cook sausages over it in an army dixie. Then we'd beg a stale loaf or two at Grannie Grieves's bakery and make what would be known to a later generation as hot dogs. Ronnie and I were deputed to do this. Of course we had no sausages, but everyone bought an occasional length of 'butcher's sausage,' as we called the long coil that lay piled on an enormous plate on every counter, and throughout the week we all snapped a few inches off and smuggled them in our none-too-clean handkerchiefs to Lily, who stored them in a basin under the mangle and covered it with a tin plate to keep the cats off.

What to sell presented the next problem. We weren't girls and couldn't cook jam tarts and things like that. We collected vast piles of comics—*Rovers, Wizards, Adventures, Champions,* and the like, and everyone brought a toy he'd got tired of. Sam's mother made us a bedroom jug of lemonade from a packet of crystals, and we used clean one-pound jam-jars to drink from. Fred wrote hundreds of lines for the few grammar-school types who might come and were always glad of reserves for future impositions. He chose 'Bells of Shandon' because its lines were the shortest in the book. I helped him and together we chanted:

'Whose sounds so wild would,
In days of childhood,
Fling round my cradle,
Their magic spells,'

as we knocked them off at twopence a hundred.

Winnie and Gladys turned co-operative after all, and made us a couple of trays of pink nutty toffee.

And Lily offered all she had—herself. It was arranged that she would sell kisses to all comers at a penny each, and a roaring trade was expected. Lily's kisses were popular and famous. That was how she rewarded us when we played schools for getting all our sums right. Unfortunately, being no good at arithmetic, I had never qualified, but by the Saturday of the bazaar I had amassed fourpence by fetching coal from the local depot in an iron-shod wheelbarrow to four old couples who had no children to send. We all bought our coal that way—a hundredweight at a time—except the rich across the park. They sometimes bought a ton at once—it cost a whole pound! I had never kissed any of the girls except Winnie, who tasted of gob-stoppers and was inclined to dribble, so I was rather looking forward to Lily's which were said to be as long and expert as Vilma Banky's in a Valentino film.

The day of the bazaar was bright and clear, much to our satisfaction. It was bitterly cold, but the ice soon melted on the pools between the cobbles. We got our 'messages' over as soon as possible—coal, and pillow slips of bread from the Co-op, and saveloys and pease-pudding for Saturday's dinner, and half a stone of Lilywhite flour for Sunday's baking.

Then to Wilson's yard to set out our bazaar. Ronnie and I lighted our fire Scout fashion and put our sections of sausage into the dixie. The table was piled high with comics and tarnished toys and toffee. On the back door Lily had chalked, 'Grand Football Bazaar. Opening at 2 p.m.', and Rinso had put notices in four or five of the little house-shops we had at every street corner. In any case, the news had spread to all the neighbouring streets and round school and by half past one a pushing mob was filling the back lane and yelling for admission. The smell of frying sausages wafted out to their eager noses. Ronnie sliced the stale bread with some difficulty. His Scout knife was a bit blunt after chopping up the orange boxes.

Lily, in a pink blouse (she must have been frozen), took up her stance by the lavatory door. This was the only place where kisses could be exchanged in privacy and a suitable semi-darkness.

With an innate fastidiousness she had sprinkled herself with Devon Violets and burned sprays of lavender in her bower.

Rinso stood at the table mounting guard over an empty bait-can which we hoped to fill with the accumulated pocket money of a dozen streets in the next hour. He nodded to Fred and the door was unbolted. Like a barbarian horde the customers surged in—and made straight for Lily.

An hour later it was all over, and we were sitting round the red ashes of our cooking fire, dipping pieces of stale bread into the still sizzling dregs of sausage fat. The lemonade jug was empty. Abandoned jam-jars littered the yard. Not a comic, not a toy, not a lump of toffee was left. Lily, dishevelled but triumphant, sat enthroned on the inverted rain-barrel, a Woodbine glowing between her somewhat overworked lips.

Rinso tipped the heavy bait-can on to the table-top and we counted the takings, huddled over them like a rugger scrum. It looked a lot, but there was only ten and sevenpence, three French pennies, a token that said 'Long live Victoria', and an Indian coin of doubtful value.

Would this buy a ball, a real case ball, splendid and brown and leather-smelling, with a lace to tighten and beautiful stitched panels?

Rinso shook his head sadly. We were five shillings short —a lot of money then.

'Can't ye buy a bladder,' suggested Winnie, 'and get the case later?' Rinso shook his head again. We'd done this before and the bladder had lasted only three days. It could not survive our vigorous bootings against the gable end where a faded poster said 'Hang the Kaiser'.

'We must get this last five bob,' said Rinso as if it were a trivial sum. All eyes turned to Lily, but sixty more favours were rather a lot to ask, and in any case where could customers be found at this late hour when pocket money had all been spent?

I still had my fourpence, but this didn't seem the time to press Lily in any sense, so I slipped it regretfully into the can.

Grimly, hands thrust in pockets, we slouched up the street looking rather hopelessly for lost coins that eager customers might have dropped in the gutters. Mrs. Reed passed us clutching her great bundle of Sunday clothes with a clock shaped like Napoleon's hat sticking out of the top. Regularly every Monday she pawned these things for the rent, and regularly every Saturday afternoon she got them back again for a brief twenty-four hours of Sunday respectability.

We took no notice of her, but Lily drew Winnie aside and they ran off back to Lily's house. The rest of us hung about in the bitter east wind dribbling a stone round one another, full of disappointment.

'So near and yet so far,' muttered Ronnie, as Rinso jingled the takings in his pocket.

A door slammed down the street and Lily and Winnie were running back towards us. Lily carried a brown-paper parcel. 'Howway,' she said firmly, 'I've had an inspiration.'

We followed her down into town to an alley near the school clinic where the shop was that we were looking for. Its three dirty brass balls glinted in the dusk. In the window were watches and rings and china jugs, and worn navy suits, and pictures of Highland cattle—all the sad debris of improvident homes.

We looked at them while the girls were inside. In a few minutes they came out again, Lily pale but triumphant.

'We're all right, lads,' she said, 'he's give us five bob on them.'

'What on, Lily?' I asked seeing she was upset.

'Me silver dancing shoes,' she replied, turning away to hide her tears. 'I've only worn them once to the Mechanics' Dance.'

'We'll get them back for you, Lily,' promised Rinso, as we hurried round to the leather shop, but we knew, and so did she, that we never would.

What made her do it? Love, I suppose. Love for Rinso, who hadn't even kissed her that afternoon and probably never would. His eyes were only for the ball, which he bounced all the way home, and his mind on the team he would be able to train, and how we would beat Raleigh Street at last and with our own ball on some not too distant Saturday.

And we did. I even remember the score, 4—2. This isn't because I scored a goal. I've never done that in my life, but because it was the day Lily got her dancing shoes back.

Somehow I was the only one in the street that afternoon when she came running up.

'Guess what, Barty!' she said excitedly. 'Me da's three-horse roller's come up and he's give us five bob.'

I remembered Sports Day far back in the summer when her own fleetness had won her the original price of her beloved shoes.

Together we went down the street to the pawnship, past the Mechanics' where a poster said 'Select Dance Tonight', and Lily took in her preciously preserved ticket and came out with them under her arm.

On our way back, as the first gas lamps flickered into life and threw their wan pools of radiance on the already frosty pavements, she took my arm suddenly and steered me into a narrow lane between the Co-op dairy and a chemist's. The boys had been right about Lily's kisses. They were nothing at all like poor Winnie's. It was like drowning in the nicest possible way.

And when we emerged into the teatime street, and she took my hand in hers and we ran together over the railway bridge and back to our street where the ball was being punted about between lamps by Rinso and Ronnie and the rest, I was more than football crazy.

May and December

THE first thing I heard that May morning forty years ago was a lark singing. That and the flapping of a sheet someone had left out to dry in the back lane. And soon there was the milk-horse stamping on the cobbles and my mother opening the door to take her jug in. These sounds were perennial, there was nothing odd about them. What was different this morning was their intensity. You could hear them distinctly—every throb of the aspiring bird, each rasp of the pony's impatient hoof. The generalised background roar made by ten miles of shipyards, foundries, pits and factories on both sides of the Tyne (all lumped together as 'the works' by my mother) that dominated and half obliterated all our domestic sounds was missing.

There were voices in the street, too, not just of women going through the daily ritual of step-stoning, but men's.

'It's like Armistice Day!' I heard Bob Major shout across. Now did he mean the first one, I wondered, when he lay in his front-line trench waiting for it all to be over, or those we knew when everything stopped except people coughing, and you waited tensely for the first hoarse notes of the Durham Light Infantry bugles? Certainly a similar excitement was in the air, a similar expectancy. The great General Strike had begun.

At breakfast my mother, deprived of her usual *Daily Mail*, was trying to get a news bulletin on my crystal set. As I gobbled bread and milk and fried bread, she jabbed with the reluctant cat's whisker, but all that came through was fragmentary Morse from the coastguard station and bits of a Chopin étude played by the resident pianist.

I left her waiting for some message of hope from Mr. Baldwin, and looking like an elderly anxious ship's operator, when Fred knocked for me. Strapless satchel under my arm, crammed with unread books, I legged it with Fred, similarly burdened, across the park and up the railway line. There were no trains to look out for today, and no precarious half-mile of joy-riding on the buffers, and though we did not yet know it, those lines would rust and grow grass over them until next winter.

Northwards the gantry cranes were still and silent, and southwards the pithead wheels were idle on Boldon Hill. Fred was in a jubilant mood, bawling 'Cushy Butterfield', and shoving me into a display outside a fruit shop. His strong but simple sense of humour was apt to express itself that way.

I didn't feel as pleased about the General Strike as Fred did, but then his father was a militant I.L.P. man, a shipyard carpenter one remove from mining stock, and claiming some remote kinship with Tommy Hepburn, their Victorian strike hero, whose grave in Heworth churchyard was still said to be tended by devout old miners. They were going to have plenty of time to tend it, I thought uncharitably, as we ran down the last warm deserted road to where the school, decent Georgian brick, basked in the kind morning sun.

My father was dead after several years of unemployment. The steelworks had not waited until this May morning to close. They had failed soon after the Armistice and the last of my father's pay cheques—still hanging threaded on a rusty wire over his wooden armchair—was dated 1920.

At school the atmosphere was one of noise and excitement, but beneath it I soon sensed a strong element of hostility, or rather, two conflicting elements. It stood in an outer suburb, surrounded by decent houses, and more than half our pupils came from them. The rest lived in the real town on the riverward side of the dividing railway. Fred and I came from a little no-man's-land of streets, respectable but far from posh, and named after Empire-guarding admirals.

The suburbs were anti-strike, and pro-Baldwin, Canterbury, and Churchill; the town pretty solidly behind the miners and A. J. Cook, swayed by memories of Black Friday and the simple humanity of 'Not a penny off the pay, not a minute on the day'.

We tried to ascertain the sympathies of the staff by a study of their platform faces during prayers, but without success. Hunter's wore its habitual atheist's sneer, and Stone's his wet warm-hearted grin. One or two men were absent, said to be driving buses or food lorries.

The girls began to get soppy about them (they were obviously the younger men) and ardent feminine glances awarded posthumous decorations to their empty chairs. At least Fred hoped they would be posthumous. He expressed himself with a Saxon pith and brevity less common then, about Tories, the bourgeoisie, and idealistic schoolmasters. There wasn't much I could say either. His father had the M.M. and had been gassed twice.

In the schoolyard angry and ill-instructed groups were vociferous at morning break. A fight broke out between black-browed handsome Jimmy Dennis, whose father was said to be a Communist, and Arnold, the son of a mine manager. The latter had tramped six miles to school from somewhere beyond Windy Nook, and was feeling deservedly pleased with himself, and a bit of a Conservative martyr.

Mr. Hall, one-armed since Loos and therefore grudgingly respected by us all, broke it up.

'Who's right, sir?' asked little Gascoigne, hot for certainties. Mr. Hall, shrugged, and Roche, our form Lothario, lit a Passing Cloud behind his retreating back and drawled, ' "A plague on both your houses",' but as we were all doing *Romeo and Juliet* for the Oxford it wasn't all that devastating.

School finished early I remember on that far-away afternoon, to allow the people who usually came by train to go their varying ways home, and at three o'clock Fred and I were walking down the long road towards town and the silence.

There was nothing to see in the suburbs except a solitary mounted policeman jogging along on his chestnut horse. I remember that its shining rump was covered with a drift of laburnam petals which were falling from front garden trees, and that the rider was whistling, a little incongruously, 'Save your sorrow for tomorrow', a current dance band hit of the time.

Once over the station bridge, however (deserted for once

even by Tim, a ragged Irish half-wit who had lived under its draughty cover ever since I could remember), we were in a different town. There was shouting and singing outside the Engineer's Arms and the Rolling Mill Tavern which had not long closed. A bus passed—one of the private home-made sort we had then, full of blackleg miners in their tell-tale dirt. Every window had been broken, but more stones were thrown, though in a half-hearted manner.

In one street the road was deep in what seemed to be snow. A man was nursing a broken head and a pub-happy crowd were pushing his lorry down the slope to the boat-landing, followed by legions of yelling children.

'Cement,' said Fred briefly. 'They're only supposed to shift food, Barty. Bloody black-legs.'

We were now in a quarter of the town solidly and necessarily Labour, an early Victorian slum named by some scholarly factory-owning alderman after the metaphysical poets. I wondered if any of the rough barefoot girls clad only in dirty frocks or the boys in their jerseys slashed like proletarian doublets, would ever hear of Donne and Traherne and Crashaw, whose half-obliterated names adorned their tenements.

At fifteen I felt a certain social and intellectual superiority to these 'down the street' children—all the more ironical, I suppose, because to an outsider Fred and I, with our over-patched shoes, dyed ex-army coats, and frayed inky collars, would have seemed only a very little different.

Several lorries were bobbing about in the Tyne among the moored sculler-boats, like odd swimming animals. Over on the Northumberland side, scaffolding round half-built ships rose up like a bare winter forest. One lonely hammer rang somewhere and a jet or two of steam escaped from a dormant power station. All along the boat-landing workmen strolled, sprawled, or sat, hands thrust in overall front pockets, not knowing what to do with this sudden and important liberty.

One or two drunks slept on draughty seats, and coming back through the town again, a dozen idle apprentices were chanting 'Land of Hope and Glory' with unmelodious irrelevance to the accompaniment of a harmonica. Behind them Sir Charles Mark Palmer, in bird-spattered free-stone, gazed with blind serenity across the town he had put on the industrial map nearly a century before. I wondered what he would think of this strike, and if, as Fred hoped, it was really the beginning of a revolution.

Tim was back at his post on the station steps grimacing enviously at a shabby old man who was selling copies of *Billy's Weekly Liar*, his bulbous nose gripped by a pair of pince-nez fastened too far down for them to be of any use as aids to seeing. What little money Tim earned he got by carrying bags, and now that there were no trains, he would be destitute as long as the strike lasted.

Fred and I separated at the top of Grenville Street (he lived in Marne Avenue then, on a new estate) and went our separate ways to write up Charles's Law and prepare a chapter of Daudet. Things like that seemed to go on in spite of national crises.

There was a good smell of frying sausages as I ran upstairs, and the fire was bright on the gilded Mazzawattee tea-caddy and my Treaty of Versailles 'peace pot'. My mother was listening in again and nodding assent with a pleased smile to everything Mr. Baldwin or whoever it was was saying. There was no doubt where her sympathies lay, with her twenty years in service and her medieval trust in a paternal aristocracy.

I felt baffled and miserable for the next nine days, drawn so much to the gay good-humoured students in their leather-patched jackets, driving our trains and buses with such dash and inefficiency; and I was unhappy about the pickets, stoning with harsh obscenities, black-leg miners and their posses of baton-waving police. Fred and I were quite cool towards one another by the time it was over.

'You're nowt but a bloody master's man!' he cried furiously, as deep in some interminable social wrangle we passed the lane ends where stocky men, lean as their nervy whippets, spat into the summer dust. For the miners, of course, didn't go back. The spoil-heap grew green like a delectable mountain, above the fields where their ponies rolled and gambolled and fought all through our summer holidays and on into open-skied chilly autumn. Their children were hungry, shoeless, half forgotten by the prosperous part of the town. They said nothing, and, if they had, the river roar would have drowned it.

As the weather got colder we made duff-balls on the pit-heap to eke out our stolen wood. The bridge to the park was soon reduced to its basic metal skeleton. People took to going to bed early, but, as Bob Major lewdly said, that would have its disadvantages come next June. Soon there were rumours of a return to work. Fred indignantly denied them. But one November morning he called for me and I saw the defeat in his face.

'They've gone back, Barty,' he said, all his confidence and aggression drained away.

We saw some of them coming down the grass-grown

railway track as we doubled up it to inevitable school. I was ashamed to look at their jaunty hollow faces, to meet the hostile eyes of those cruelly broken men. One, only a boy, whistled a defiant tune and slashed thistle heads off as he passed us.

By pure chance we sang 'Fight the good fight' that morning, and heard through it the long-silent pit buzzer on Boldon Hill. The last verses were sung with twice the usual vigour, and some of us knew what we were singing about. Fred kept his eyes well down, but I saw a tear splash on his dirty boot and I suddenly knew, in spite of my middle-of-the-road temperament, whose side I would be on for the rest of my life.

By chance, the last evening of that bitter strike year stands out vividly in my memory, both because it marked the end (technically at any rate) of a bad time, and because on that evening I went to see *Broken Biscuits*, my first-ever revue.

Perhaps the proximity of Tyneside to Scotland had something to do with it, but we always made a great thing of New Year in our town. Some of my Scots schoolmates would make their annual pilgrimage to Newcastle to see the beginning of 1927 under the triple lantern of St. Nicholas's Cathedral and join in the raucous singing and bottle-smashing that started as the bells began to ring their triumphant peal above the dark river.

I didn't go, but I remember coming to like New Year better than Christmas. Perhaps this was because one of the childish things I was putting away at that time was my religion. I was glad to get all the church-going and carol-singing out of the way, and looked forward, now I'd outgrown Jesus and Father Christmas to the more uncomplicated and purely secular pleasures of New Year's Eve.

My mate at that time was a boy named Bill Robson. He lived in the mining area of our town. You opened his cottage door straight from the wet cold street and immediately you were met by a blast of hot air from the fire—one of those never-dying pit-cottage fires where nothing but the best gleddy coal burned day and night throughout the year. Very likely his father would be sitting in the zinc bath and splashing soap over the fireside clippy mat. He would be spelling out the day's racing while his pint pot of tea stood on the hob within easy reach, and Spark and her son Snap, his two precious whippets, lay full stretch on the only upholstered chair.

When I lifted the sneck and walked in Snap would lick me all over, and Spark, having drawn back her top lip over a set of wicked yellow teeth, would modify her automatic snarl to a kind of dour grunt of appreciation, and give one condescending switch of her tail.

I went to the Robsons' house every night at that time. Bill and I sat next to one another at school, and by a simple dishonest and plausible division of labour I did the French and English homework while he attended to our maths and chemistry. Fred and I still came and went together, but he had taken to working hard and was now in a higher form.

Mr. Robson never took much notice of me. When his wife had scrubbed his blue-black back he dried, dressed, and went off to the Beehive for the evening. Mrs. Robson was fond of me because I was Bill's friend, and not rough, and (my mother having been an ex-upper servant) what she called admiringly 'a lovely talker'.

The Gem, where this first revue I ever saw was 'on', was a small music hall about five minutes away from St. Rollox Street where the Robsons lived. Revues with odd titles—sometimes mildly bawdy ones like *The Bare Idea*—came and went there frequently, but I had never been to one before. In fact my experience of the theatre was very limited. Uncle Jim, a demon for culture, had once walked us to Newcastle to hear (you could hardly call it 'see') *La Bohème* at the Theatre Royal. Tiny figures moved to and fro below us and a Welsh tenor (Ben Williams I think) had sung about Mimi's small frozen hand; and once I'd walked the other way all on my own to South Shields to see the Denville Stock Company do *Lady Windermere's Fan*. Here for a shilling I'd been able to sit right in front, and I had felt almost part of the paste-board drawing room where Oscar's epigrams flashed to and fro.

When the lights went up a tough merchant seaman next to me had said, with simple nautical wonder, 'By, son, the lives these toffs lead, eh?' It was to be many years before I found that they weren't all as witty as Wilde had made them seem.

We approached the Gem through gas-lit noisy streets, where children skipped and drunks were already slithering over the frosty cobbles. Mysie Sparkes, a schoolmate, a year or two older than Bill and me, a girl of ample charms and great good nature was coming out of a chip shop.

'Gie' us a one,' said Bill half-heartedly, but to our surprise she opened up the delicious steaming packet and let us take quite a few. Mysie was all poshed up and reeking of some exotic scent, and below her winter coat (plum was the colour that year I think) gleamed her obvious

Christmas present, a pair of the then popular Russian boots.

'Are you going to the Gem?' I managed to ask. To speak to a girl like Mysie was an achievement for me.

'No, old man,' she said, with a very fair parody of my accent, 'I'm going for a stroll on the golf-course.'

'But it's dark!' I said naively, not remembering that those blessed thirty acres between the slag-heap and a flooded quarry where we fished for trout in summer were as populated as Hyde Park with lovers on dark winter nights.

Clutching her chips with one hand, Mysie gave me a friendly shove with the other and a quick warm smile. My innocent remark had been mistaken for wit.

It cost sixpence, if I remember rightly, to sit in the front seats of the music hall. Behind us the less affluent elbowed one another on wooden benches. Upstairs the seats were blue plush with little brass ashtrays, but they were a shilling and beyond our means, since we had bought a packet of Little Queens, a long-forgotten cigarette, but our favourite brand at that time.

All around us we could hear oranges being enjoyed—rather like the sound of footsteps crossing a swamp. The already warm air smelled of sweat and face-powder, and under the reeking oranges the faint bitter smell of monkey nuts in the mass. Now and again we got a blast from a foul clay pipe or a whiff of fried fish. Suddenly through the blue haze of smoke I caught sight of moving figures and the flash of a silver cornet. A moment later the orchestra (there were only six of them) were drowning our expectant uproar with 'Save your sorrow for to-morrow'—the tune the mounted policeman had hummed in far-off May on the first day of the strike.

Up went the curtain, covered with its homely ads for local sausage and reliable plumbers, and a gorgeously lit background of Renaissance Venice appeared, in front of which twelve young women, differing slightly as to shape and size, but equal in the brevity of their costumes and very nearly so in the timing with which they flashed their long white legs at us, sang in strange sharp Cockney voices. The third from the left was distinctly pretty, and before long Bill and I were a little in love with her. We tolerated the rest of the acts, living for the moment when the orchestra would strike up some sprightly number and the girls reappear from one or other of the wings with their untiring agility and automatic smiles.

'Each chap thinking,' I muttered to Bill, parodying a verse of Houseman we'd been learning at school, 'the smile was held for him.' And held they certainly were for much of the next two hours. Meanwhile comedians, accordion-players, jugglers and tap-dancers came and went. Only two of the many turns really stand out in my memory: an Apache dance, the first I had ever seen, where a kind of continental sewer-man alternately spurned and caressed his waif-like partner (number three of the chorus, again to our delight).

Halfway through it a broad female voice behind us was heard to complain loudly, 'Yon feller wants to make up his bloody mind!'

The other was a dim-lit Italian scene where a soprano concealed in a rickety tower sang a passionate duet with a tenor in a purple velvet doublet. A hush fell on the house, for both singers had the remains of good voices, and their duet was, of course, the renunciation scene from

Il Trovatore—known to most of the audience, though less as an incident in an opera than an overture played in the park by all the local prize silver bands.

Then back to comedy again, and a red-faced little man who wheeled a pram rapidly to and fro across the stage shouting, 'Hoi! Hoi! Hoi!' He must surely have done more than that, but Bill and I were waiting for the chorus girls and didn't pay him much attention.

At the end of the show a lady clad in black with small brilliant things like fish-scales all over her dress, a triple rope of pearls, and a duchessy accent, thanked us all from the bottom of her heart, wished us a happy and prosperous 1927 (some hopes!), and told us in coy confidence that such was the financial success of *Broken Biscuits* that she was no longer a 'broken' biscuit.

Then the exit doors slammed open and we crunched our way out over a sea of monkey-nut shells. We took a long look back, loath to leave the bright lights and plushy warmth, and face the cold streets again, but at least it was New Year's Eve and restlessness and excitement were in the air.

We could hear people dumping their ashes and other refuse in bins and middens, for the tradition was still strong on Tyneside then that nothing was ever taken out on New Year's Day. That was a time for bringing in—beginning, of course, at midnight, when the dark-haired first-foot would give his ritual knock and enter with gifts of coal and bread and salt.

That moment was drawing near, but as both Bill and I were fair, our services weren't in demand, so we took the dogs for a run on the golf-course. A thin moon threw some light on the frosty turf. Bill went some hundred yards away towards the quarry where a night bird was crying intermittently. I stood and fluttered an old silk scarf kept for the purpose, and first Spark, and then Snap, and then both together, raced silently like ghost dogs through the eerie light and took it neatly from my rather nervous hands. Spark was inclined to take it a bit close to your fingers.

Just before twelve we went back to St. Rollox Street, where outside the Beehive a knot of tipsy pitmen were anticipating 1927 and hoping with blasphemous fervour that it would be better than 1926. As many of them had only been back at work since November, when winter and hunger had broken their spirit, most felt that any change must be for the better. They shook our hands with fuddled solemnity. 'Many of them, son,' said a small emaciated man, offering us each a sup of brandy from a little flat bottle. It was very different from the familiar ginger wine that was all we teetotallers ever got. 'I hope the future holds more for you that wors did at your age,' he added optimistically.

I wondered what it would hold. We would leave school in far-off July, of course, and start work somewhere along the river—silent tonight but visible at the end of every long descending street of diminishing lamps. It was a sobering thought, almost counteracting the spoonful of brandy which had been giving me a pleasant feeling of recklessness. Twelve began striking from the clock on St. Oswald's and we all joined hands and sang, advancing and retreating again and again over the slippery cobbles. All around first-foots were hammering on doors and voices were crying 'Many of them.'

There was laughter and kissing, and, not perhaps so

oddly, here was Mysie Sparkes again on her way home from the golf-course date, and ready to spare us the remnant of a passionate evening.

Was she, almost a woman already, touched by our youth and timidity? At any rate she took us each in turn and enfolded us in her warm arms, and oh the smell of her hair and her face-powder and the long exciting taste of her kiss. It was all mixed up with the clashing bells and my already fading memory of number three in the chorus of *Broken Biscuits*.

Tug-boats hooted on the river as I hurried home through emptying streets. I remember the excitement of its being 1927 and the delicious sense of being young and feeling that it was all before me, and yet of not being equal to whatever life might demand.

The cold struck up sharply through my thin-soled shoes, but my heart was high with the passionate hope of some impossibly happy future, of which a faint foolish distillation remains even today whenever I hear distant bells at midnight 'ringing in the new'.

Trust the Gentlemen

WHEN Fred saw the horse soldiers he spat into the gutter. It was a gesture of insolent defiance. I did hope they hadn't noticed, and from their seats high in creaking saddles they probably hadn't.

What were two schoolboys walking an empty road to them?

They were fighting an east wind too, that blew all the way from Germany across the Slacks (a dreary open back-water of the Tyne) and screaming seagulls wheeled in front of their horses. One shied across the wet cobbles and Fred's eyes lit up. I could see he hoped a rider would be thrown, but he was unlucky. The line wavered, recovered, and then they were gone, striking sparks out of the road all the way to Tyne Dock, and leaving a warm smell of horse and leather on the freezing January air. Fred spat again, this time for my benefit.

'I hate soldiers, Barty,' he said apologetically. He was apologetic because he knew my father had been a soldier and was now dead. I often cleaned the bars on his silver South African War medal and wondered what it had been like at Magersfontein and Tugela Heights. He had been the sort of soldier Fred meant, a soldier from choice.

Fred exempted from his fierce generalisation all those

who had served in the Great War—now six years over—and who only remembered Loos and the Somme as some dreadful dream. It was people like my father who were 'the paid lackeys of a Tory state' Fred hoped soon to see swept away.

I could tell by his face, and by the way he kept looking across the wide expanse of water full of rotten timber baulks that looked like great scattered piano keys now that each was coated with white frost, that he was thinking of Jobling again. He always did when we came this way.

Somewhere over there, beyond the derelict shipyard and a handful of dirty-white cottages, Jobling's gibbet had stood less than a hundred years before. Soldiers had guarded that too, probably clattering along the river road just as these had done who were now bobbing midgets a mile away. Now and again their hoof-beats came with the wind like a stick drawn along railings, until the Shields tram swayed into view and drowned every sound except the gulls in its grinding roar. 'He never done it, Barty!' said Fred, not needing to explain that it was Jobling he was talking about. Striking Tyneside miners were Fred's heroes at that time. He was steeped in their history, their songs and their bitter courageous insolence. Actually his father was a shipyard carpenter, and he knew few of the closed mining community, but his romantic devotion was all the stronger for that.

'You think it was Armstrong then?' I asked for about the hundredth time.

'I'm sure it was,' said Fred, vehemently, 'he hit Nicholas Fairless before Jobling could stop him, but it was Jobling they found on Shields beach, and it was Jobling they hung.'

'Hanged,' I thought automatically; only pictures are 'hung'—but I knew better than to correct Fred.

The two men, Jobling and Armstrong, were unemployed miners, and one of them had murdered a magistrate—a grim Judge Jeffreys sort of chap—just about where Fred and I were standing now. They hanged Jobling at Durham and gibbeted his body by the river. Local tradition says it was the last time this grim rite was carried out in England, but I believe several towns claim this dubious honour. In spite of a military guard both body and gibbet had disappeared one night, to the jubilation of the local pit people.

'Howway, let's get the tram,' I said recklessly as it approached. We had no coats on and it was freezing weather.

'Where d'you think they put Jobling?' I asked, after we'd paid the conductor our reluctant pennies.

'"Full fathom five thy father lies",' quoted Fred with a better-tempered grin now we were out of the searching wind. 'I think they rowed him out to sea in a sculler and heaved him overboard.'

I thought of poor Jobling's pitch-covered body drifting above the coaly bed of the grey North Sea, and of the grim triumph there'd have been in those cottages we were racketing past, where old Irishwomen sat at their doors now on summer evenings, bowing to passers-by and clicking their rosaries. The miners had lived there then until they were evicted, and then they'd camped on the bleak salt grass across the road from Bede's monastery. I was busy with a private daydream where he and his monks moved among the wretched makeshift tents distributing food and comforts to the dispossessed, when Fred's elbow dug into my ribs.

'Howway, wake up, Barty! Terminus!'

We got out unwillingly into the evening street. Gas lamps were yellow and frost stars flickered on the pavements. Among the posters at the lane end advertising Stewart Rome and Pola Negri one said: 'Vote for . . .' but a rival party hand had ripped the offending name away. I could see by the colour that it was the Labour candidate's.

'—— vandals!' muttered Fred with an unquotable epithet. He took out a pencil and began to put the name in again in big letters. I was glad when he'd finished because the works were coming out and some impatient Liberal riveter or Tory plater could easily have clouted him into the gutter. It was the eve of the first 1924 election and feelings ran high.

'See ye half past six,' said Fred, handing me a bundle of leaflets when we separated at the top of Grenville Street to go home to tea.

My heart missed a beat. I'd promised to go with him to give out last-minute admonitions to vote Labour in the toughest part of town, and my mother was a staunch and blinkered Tory. She wasn't very pleased about my mild addiction to Socialism. The company of the great, and life in houses where Tennyson read his poetry to the old Queen and Lord Kitchener was likely to call, had done nothing to fit her for the rough life of a shipyard town on the Tyne. The hands that had rocked several infant lords to sleep and placed soup discreetly before the last Czar of all the Russias could hardly be expected to handle what she thought of as Bolshevik propaganda. All through tea she kept looking at the pile of innocent literature as though it might conceal some sort of bomb.

The candle flame (I suppose we hadn't a shilling for the new electric light) flickered on the brass-topped clock, and on my late father's portrait above the mantelpiece. People said he looked like Lord Randolph Churchill, but he'd been a Liberal like 'that young fool Winston,' as he said half affectionately, half aggressively, according to whether he was remembering the Boer War or the Dardenelles.

'Trust the gentlemen,' said my mother gently. She always had and always would. But 'Vote! Vote! Vote! for Mr. Whoever-it-was,' chanted the children as Fred and I crossed the bridge over the railway that divided our semi-suburb from the gas-lit uproar of the real town.

There were gangs of them everywhere, marching in fours as their ex-soldier teachers had taught them to do, and swinging bombaters—balls of tough paper on string, sometimes with a stone in the centre—and singing again and again their tireless four lines of doggerel. Unlike to-day there was plenty of life in the streets then at seven o'clock on a winter's evening. Most of the shops were still open. The many pubs poured their brassy brilliance out on to the frosty streets every time a swing door opened. The smell of beer and thick waves of tobacco smoke drifted out too, and dispersed in the biting air. Greatly daring, Fred opened one forbidden door and hurled a handful of his propaganda at the astonished drinkers. We fled (though no one would have thought it worth while to pursue us) past the Penny Bazaar and the steamy aromatic pork shop, and dived into a coal-black entry between Lipton's and the Meadow Dairy, Voices muttered in the dark, and someone struck a match lighting up an evil face for a moment. Hard hands seized us.

'Where ye goin', son?' There was no tenderness in the epithet.

'Taking out election leaflets,' said Fred in a strangulated voice.

Cruel hands were tightening his muffler.

'Who for, son?' This was menacing.

Fred gasped out the name of his candidate just in time.

'Lucky for you, son,' said our invisible interlocutor.

We were set free and propelled with half-hearted kicks down the alley and out into the private world of Poets' Corner. This was a handful of streets between the main shopping territory and the river, a Victorian slum where I had been only once before, and that by day, taking Harvest Festival fruit and vegetables to one or two decent old women who sometimes came to St. Stephen's.

I remember a house of indescribable smells and heart-breaking crying, where every room was let to a family. On the landing stood a broken chair with a dirty tin bowl full of foul water on it where everybody washed.

My old lady lay on a broken-down bed under a pile of dirty harn. There was nothing else in the room. Some obscure likeness to my mother in her South Country voice as she raised her flushed face from the straw pillow to thank me had touched even my selfish young heart. Was this where you got to from trusting the gentlemen? Fred would have thought so, I knew, as we shoved our leaflets through battered letter-boxes, feeling for them in the semi-darkness between wind-tossed lop-sided lamps.

' "No light, but rather darkness visible",' chuckled Fred. We were doing *Paradise Lost*, Books 1 and 2, that term.

I thought of school, hardly more than a mile away, in a different world of quiet streets and privet hedges and Clementi's sonatas on the front-room piano, and I was glad when we were done and emerged from the last alley onto an east-winded water-front.

Behind us the Poets' Corner kids, ragged and bootless to a man, marched and chanted. Someone in the lighted bar-room of the Golden Fleece was singing—if you could call it that—'The Rose of Tralee'. The inn sign creaked crazily, and if you listened carefully you could hear the tide lapping against the boat-landing, and the rhythmic thud of the approaching ferry-boat's engines. Her twin red and green lights moved up and down on the dark water in front of the fixed stars of the Northumberland side's galaxy of cranes.

We clung together in the great gusts that threatened to blow us off the quayside, smelling driftwood and iron and paint, and the poverty behind us, and now and again, very faint and elusive, the salt North Sea.

When St. Stephen's clock struck ten we slid all the way home on the black treacherous ice that had formed on exposed pavements.

'Tomorrow, Barty,' said Fred jubilantly, meaning less our inevitable meeting than the election of which he hoped so much. But, 'Trust the gentlemen,' murmured my mother with exasperating fidelity, as she stirred my cocoa and the kettle sang for the stone hot-water bottle that would warm my cold lineny bed.

Election Day wasn't as exciting as we'd hoped. There weren't many stones thrown, and if there were fights, it was after we were safe in bed. We had to wait until the following day for the results. They might have been on the wireless, but I'd broken my cat's whisker with impatient jabbing. I woke with a start to hear a boy crying the *North Mail* with more than usual insistence. His bare feet went 'slap, slap' past our open door where my mother was busy with the daily ritual of doing the step. The harsh sound of the rubbing stone stopped, and she came in holding the paper between a soapy finger and thump. One look at her face told me.

'Poor Mr. Baldwin,' was all she said.

I had a mental picture of him drifting away with his pipe and pigs. The first ever Labour Government was in, and handsome Ramsay MacDonald was coming down from Scotland like a latter-day Prince Charlie.

'We've done it, Barty!' shouted Fred, walking the town like a conqueror. His enthusiastic eyes saw the shut steelworks flare into life and Poets' Corner obliterated.

My mother, on the other hand, thought that we would need military protection any day, though she conceded that Mr. MacDonald was good-looking and might even be literate. I was, as usual, fatally middle-of-the-road, now burning with social indignation like Fred, now regretting what we all thought were my mother's 'last sad squires'.

Once again, the day before school started, we walked along by the Slacks. The posters were looking sorry already. Soon they would soak in February rains and in March they'd all be blown away. The sun shone on gently lifting timber baulks as the tide came silently in. The seagulls were farther out and muted. Away, beyond the tanker moving slowly down to sea, a riveter's hammer sounded like a distant woodpecker in the bare forest of staging. It was almost warm.

'School tomorrow, Barty,' said Fred with a rueful grin.

We stood looking out over the shining mud-flats for a minute. He glanced across at where we thought the old gibbet must have stood and I know he was thinking, 'Jobling justified at last.'

I was glad afterwards that he'd had his moment and didn't know that autumn was to bring the fatal forged Zinoviev letter, and a return of the gentlemen, and a reprieve for Poets' Corner that was to last another twenty long and bitter years.

Open Day

EVERY morning the slides were folded back after the registers had been called, and the whole school formed an inward-looking hollow square—row on row of jersey-clad figures, with here and there a grey shirt and tie, and even one or two Eton collars and lop-sided bows. In the centre was the piano on which Miss Madison was playing Blake's 'Grand March'. If ever she wore anything but a green costume we never saw it, and if her face ever expressed anything but aloof disdain that was hidden from us too.

Beside her stood Mr. Macdonald, prayer book in hand, and cane under arm.

'Like a servant of the Lord,
With his bible and his sword,'

muttered Herbert Benson, being given to quotation even at the age of eleven.

Round the perimeter of this clear space of floor stood the staff, in front of us and facing inwards, but ready to swing round at the least whisper or shuffle and take your name for judgement and slaughter later on during scripture. There were eight men and four women, and we knew them intimately, their physique, clothes, and smells of tobacco, peppermint, or scrubbed virginity. They were completely known and utterly boring, like the hymn 'Through all the changing scenes of life' we would soon be singing; like the classrooms that smelled of ink and apple cores, and the wet asphalt smell of the yard across which the shadow of our Union Jack—perhaps it was Empire Day—rippled like water.

As Mr. Macdonald read the prayers we could hear the rope whipping against the flagstaff outside, and beyond the green door that led to the lobby the brisk sounds of Mr. Brand caning the lates and the occasional howl of some less than stoical soul.

It seemed to be a day like any other day, but, our devotions over, Mr. Macdonald laid both his manual and his cane on top of the piano and prepared to address us. Even then I didn't realise the importance of what he was saying. To speak to us for a few minutes after prayers wasn't all that rare—it generally meant trouble for someone caught stealing or climbing on the roof or not washing, and I automatically switched off my attention and began my favourite dream of being a buffalo-hunter.

I was just cutting tough lengths of pemmican by the smoky brushwood fire when Herbert dug me in the ribs. I turned left instead of right, face to face with Lemon Ward, who was a head taller than me and whose jersey smelled of fried bread. Mr. Charlton said 'George!' with mock despair. It was not my name, and it raised the usual half-hearted laugh. I turned right-about and we were marched off to our classroom, a high echoing chamber without a ceiling that opened off the lobby. Mr. Charlton actually shut the door and left us.

There was a moment's silence—a kind of tribute to his

ex-Northumberland Fusiliers discipline—and then pandemonium. Under it Herbert Benson and I could talk in relatively low tones.

'I wonder what it'll be like, Barty,' he said.

'Much the same as usual,' I replied, playing for time as I hadn't listened to a word.

'Ye weren't listening, Barty. How can it be much the same as usual when we've never had an Open Day before?'

'What's an Open Day?'

'Ye're a dozy beggar, Barty. D'ye never listen to owt? All wor mas and das is coming to see an exhibition of wor work on the classroom wall and there's going to be a drill display and singing and a morality play.'

'And Macdonald's coming up on the platform at the end,' shouted Lemon Ward, 'to show everybody his . . .'

'Prowess,' suggested Herbert, always ready with a pedantic word, and it saved a delicate situation for once, as Mr. Charlton and Mr. Macdonald had entered the room unnoticed under cover of the noise, and stood switching their canes tentatively, and preparing to call out the regulars who averaged four or five beatings a day and took it all in their stride. Lemon was usually one, but he escaped this time.

My mother wasn't as affected by my astonishing announcement about Open Day as one might have supposed. I knew why, of course. She was worried about money. Not just money in general—we were always worried about that, but a specific sum—five pounds to be precise, which was more than twice a labourer's wages in 1923. A cheque for this amount should have come on her birthday a week ago, and hadn't for the first time in fifteen years.

Her old master, a Lord Lieutenant of Hertfordshire, had been sending it ever since she left his demesne to marry a penniless crane-driver and exchange the quiet of the home counties where you could hear the stable clock a mile away for the shattering roar of the shipbuilding Tyne.

Now my father was dead, and another man drove his crane to and fro across the sky, and just when we needed Captain Butler's annual gift more than ever, it failed to come.

To my mother the Captain was a symbol of all her lost security of vassaldom, and I knew, hearing her tell stories of the great country house, of horses and dogs long since dead, seven-course dinners, hunt balls and the like, what pleasure and anguish my childish requests for 'something about the Captain' would give her, who had not been out of our grimy North Country town for many years. She clung fiercely to her difference, living on the memory of pines murmuring through a village evensong, and the litany of names—Pharaoh, Auster, Redcap, Blanche, Kitty, Bruce, Shot and Buzz—pointers and hunters—that cropped up so often in her stories. The money meant a lot, but being remembered meant very much more, and I added my mother's quiet distress to the list of things that worried me, and about which I prayed far into the night, without however much hope of being either heard or helped.

High on my list of priorities was this Open Day. Some aspects of it were all right—my writing and drawing weren't so bad, and Mr. Charlton had put up a piece of poetry I'd copied from the collected works of Lord Byron in the tortured copperplate we practised then, and a sketch (lined-in and shaded) of his army boots, a bowler hat, and a cottage loaf grouped together on a desk-top. And it was thrilling to think that for a whole day there wouldn't be any real lessons or canings, and that fathers and mothers would be coming and going for all the world as if school was a normal sort of place like the Co-op Hall or the Mechanics' Institute, and not a special hell reserved for teachers and pupils.

Three things bothered me: the drill display, the choir, and the play—I was in them all. I can't think why, except that perhaps as Standard V was the 'scholarship' class and I'd managed to pass this immensely important exam I'd got a false reputation for nous (of which I'd practically none) in the eyes of Mr. Macdonald.

Mr. Charlton knew it. It was especially evident in drill; Swedish drill, as it was in those days, with plenty of 'arms bend'—a curious position where the open hands rested lightly on the shoulders. I could manage this, but it was only a starting position from which one might have to shoot one's arms in any one of four possible directions.

'Upwards! *Upwards!*' he would cry warningly, 'stretch!' —only to see mine flung despairingly forwards, sideways, or even downwards. He could have dropped me, I suppose, but I became a sort of daily challenge to him. I might, I gathered, break my mother's heart but not his.

Miss Madison was concerned about my singing. I had no voice, and once she had discovered who was putting all Standard 5 out (she set us off la-laing and came round listening to us each in turn) I was allowed to sit apart and read *The Buffalo Hunters* undisturbed. But Open Day it seemed was different. I was needed, and as something called a 'second'. While the younger boys fluted 'Sweet and low, wind of the western sea', we sang something sad and minor and different. At least the others did. I stayed with them long enough to put them out and then somewhat shakily joined the dominant sopranos at 'over the ro-olling waters go' a beat or two behind.

Miss Madison sometimes slammed the piano shut and refused to continue.

At length, prompted by the resourceful Herbert, I solved the problem by whispering the words inaudibly. Things went much better then, and I could cross the choir off the list of worries.

Worst of all was the play, in which I had a large but unattractive part. Of all the possible plays in the world Mr. Macdonald had chosen *Everyman*. Its dour morality appealed no doubt to his serious Scots temperament. Its simplicity made it an easy one to stage. He had hit on the idea of splitting the single part of Everyman into two, giving the speeches to a boy and a girl alternately. This served the double purpose of bringing the opposite sex under judgement (which no doubt seemed fairer to him) and halving the learning work necessary for the main character.

I was Goods and Riches, and had quite a lot to say, but it wasn't this that worried me, as I had a prolific memory then. What did was having Hilda Martin stretch out her arms to me and her saying, 'Alas, I have loved thee all my life!'

She was a very beautiful girl from a superior part of the town—her father kept a draper's shop—and I could not meet her eye. In vain did Miss Pinkerton, Mr. Macdonald's co-producer, exhort me to lift my head up. I never saw Hilda Martin properly, and to this day would hardly know her.

The rest of the cast were made to approximate to their moral qualities. Lemon Ward with his great size and broken voice was Strength. A frail girl who looked, and probably was, in the first stages of anaemia personified Good Deeds. She was little and thin, and had a quavering voice; eminently suitable, as I gathered Everyman's Good Deeds had been few and far between.

I saw nothing ironic, however, in those days in my portraying Goods and Riches, while my genteel mother hardly opened her front door because the stair carpet existed in name only.

My jersey too was almost more darns than original material, but in the play I wore a sleeveless vest and my thin arms were ringed with bangles and bracelets collected by Miss Pinkerton from the girls' school. Round my neck I wore strings of coins, and on my head a gilded cardboard coronet.

When Hilda called 'Where art thou, my Goods and Riches?' I flung back the lid of a gold-painted trunk in which I had lain concealed until that moment, and, fixing my eyes on her feet, went into my first speech in a rapid gabble.

Unfortunately the play was too long for me to be in the trunk before it began. They'd tried that, but when I came up like a scarlet gasping Jack-in-the-Box people had rushed about for glasses of water and smelling salts. So I had to wait in the wings, and, under cover of a little dance done by Beauty, Fellowship and Kindred, nipped into the box a mere five minutes before I was due to speak. Afterwards I lay and suffocated happily until the angels blew their trumpets and the play was over.

As Open Day approached, the days grew warmer and it

was spring. Not that there was much to show for it in our town, a smell of crushed grass and daisies from the strip of garden in front of the school, green weeds thrusting up between the cobbles in back lanes, and a racket of sparrows in the early morning.

Eva, a little girl I hadn't seen all the winter, took to waiting for me again at the bottom of Maple Street—hand on hip, with her arm crooked for me to put mine through and a smile she thought was mocking, but which even I could see was uncertain and full of affection. I would rather have had Nessie Macintosh, who (naturally) wore a kilt, and who never looked my way, but I was glad someone liked me, and Eva had nice brown eyes and a mop of dark curls.

Unfortunately the spring also brought out Pratt Miller and his gang—half a dozen ragged desperadoes who ran me whenever they got the chance, which was often now that the mornings and evenings were so much lighter.

At home my mother was still waiting for her letter from the Captain. She trusted all gentlemen as a matter of course, and so did I, though I'd read enough to be a bit more worldly wise than she was. I had to have a white shirt for the drill display, and without the Captain's fiver there was no chance of getting one. She had to alter one of her own blouses and she was not a gifted needlewoman. The result hurt Mr. Charlton's military eye, but he had to make do with me. No one had a spare white shirt in those days.

On the morning of Open Day I was a bit late through waiting for the postman, but he only brought the water rate. My mother put it in the green china boot to the right of the clock and tried not to show her disappointment. I took a short cut over the brickfield, listening to the cracked school bell which would soon stop its melancholy clanking. Eva would be late too. As I jumped from tussock to tussock over this quarter of a mile of no-man's-land I thought of her waiting at the corner as long as she dared, and that was why I never saw Pratt and his minions until it was too late. They burst out from behind a great chunk of shale like the convict in *Great Expectations*, and pursued me to school yelling something I couldn't catch. Long practice in running away had given me a terrific turn of speed, and I arrived breathless but triumphant just as the bell stopped. Pratt, holding something in his hand, made a determined effort to get into the school yard, but he was driven back by half Standard 5 with lumps of coke. Mr. Macdonald, blowing his whistle, turned a Nelson eye to the throwers. Boys from other schools were fair game. Open Day began after a spectacular assembly. We sang 'Nearer my God to thee'—ruined for me by Lemon Ward, who kept hissing, 'We're sinking fast, Barty!' and making choking noises because he said the band had played it on the *Titanic*.

Later in the morning came the drill display, a fifteen-minute eternity where I managed at last to stretch my arms faultlessly in the required directions but which I eventually spoiled. This was in the *pièce de résistance*—a full knee-bend and a spot of arm-flinging while you were down there. In my relief that it was the last convolution I flung myself with such a will that I turned myself completely round and collapsed.

Mr. Charlton's breath came out like escaping steam, but the audience laughed tolerantly and when we came on dressed in our best that afternoon to sing 'Sweet and Low'

I noticed several people nudging one another and pointing me out. It was a kind of fame and my *sotto voce* singing, carried on unfortunately and only too obviously into a bar or two of dramatic rests, extended my reputation.

After this, to upset the box by jumping into it too vigorously and to be precipitated heavily among the dancers at my point of entry into *Everyman* was completely in character. The lines given to Goods are not at all funny, in fact there's not a laugh anywhere in a morality play, but as soon as I popped up, bruised and dusty, a fair-haired short-sighted boy with scrawny arms on which bangles slithered and rattled, and round whose neck strings of baubles hung like French onions, the audience began to laugh, and the louder I bawled my lines at Hilda Martin's feet, the more amused they seemed.

It took the voice of God—now a grizzled chief engineer, but then a little rather bumptious boy—to restore order.

My mother didn't know whether to laugh or cry at my triple disasters, but Mr. Macdonald, drinking his cup of tea thankfully as the school cleared of parents for many a long day, shook his head and said, 'Barton lad, you're a kinocular!'—a sure sign that his exasperation was only humorous, and I had nothing to fear tomorrow.

Eva was waiting for me. 'Don't go over the bricky,' she warned, 'I seen Pratt Miller and his lot waiting at Oak Street corner.'

We went down Holly Street, a quiet one nobody ever seemed to use, but they were waiting at the bottom of it —six of them. Pratt advanced, holding something in his dirty hand. It was a long blue envelope.

'Do yous live at 33 Grenville Street?' he asked.

'Ye know fine well he does!' snapped Eva, who was afraid of nothing.

'Well me ma says I was to give ye this,' he said, holding out the Captain's letter. 'It come by mistake to 33 Nelson a fortnight ago and I've been chasing ye with it ever since.'

He had too, but he didn't as I went home at breakneck pace with Eva to give it to my mother, and if he had, he wouldn't have caught me. Eva and I parted at the first lamp.

'I'll take ye to the Empire tomorrow,' I promised recklessly.

'It's John Gilbert in *Scaramouche*,' she said, flushing with pleasure and turning her head quickly away.

My mother was pouring the tea out as I came in, and the firelight was just beginning to be bright as the sky darkened over the roofs opposite. Her hand that took the letter trembled, and she sat holding it in pure joy all the time I was eating my baked herrings and girdle scones. Then she opened it and there was the cheque—all red and blue and important with 'Five pounds' written on it.

I sat back in my father's chair, weak with happiness. Open Day was over, and no one was really angry with me, and we were rich, and my mother was happy again, and Eva would be waiting for me in the morning, and perhaps Pratt wouldn't start chasing me for a few days.

As the darkness gathered outside, and the fire flared up cosily and shone on the dresser cups and plates, I hadn't a care in the world.

The Old Order

My father left the house at seven o'clock in the morning. I sometimes heard him clearing out the grate and lighting the fire, and with the keen nose of childhood caught the distant smell of brewing tea and frying bacon. When I got up for school, the kitchen was warm and my mother was stirring the porridge.

At half past five in the evening my father came back. He smelled of iron and oil and machinery, and he washed his hands with paraffin and dried them on cotton waste before sitting down to his tea. During the three or four hours left him before bed he did nothing—I mean nothing to help my mother. He might go out, or read *Titbits* or listen to Peter Dawson singing 'Boots' on the old gramophone, but everything he did was for himself. The eight and a half hours in the little cramped cabin of his crane high above the clash and roar of the shipyard was for us. What was left of the day belonged to him.

That was the pattern when I was a small boy. Man went forth to his work and to his labour until the evening, but woman's work was never done. My mother got up to a warm kitchen after an occasional cup of tea in bed. And that was all.

My father did not do housework, or cook, or shop, or

look after the children. He filled the coal-scuttle, chopped wood, and once a week scrubbed the backyard with a stiff broom. But those were manly outside jobs. Chivalry—and there was plenty of chivalry then, though no equality, of course—made it necessary for a man to do such things. But, oddly enough, not to help with the back-breaking job of possing on washing day, or even turning the heavy mangle.

That was left to the distaff side. I remember surprising my father turning—and rather enjoying turning—one of these antique machines. He gave me a shamefaced look and pretended to be mending a cog-wheel. My father never shopped—even his tobacco came with the groceries. His daily paper he whistled for from the front door at some bleak hour before work when the barefoot boys cried it down the street. If he wanted shoes—boots rather—shoes were for women and little children—my mother went for them; and for everything else except the suit he absolutely had to be measured for every four or five years. A man was so seldom seen in a shop in those days that a hush would fall on the place if one dared to enter, and he would be served quickly, as if every moment took something away from his masculinity.

Nor could a father push a pram. A grandfather might—just. And he would have to use one hand only and walk beside it as if it were really no concern of his. But a father who pushed his infant's chariot as I did when my children were small after the war was practically unknown.

I did know a man who cleaned his doorstep with rubby-stone like the women, and even stood back, hands on hips, to admire it. He gossiped with the housewives, saying things like 'I've done all me white things,' or 'Me bread's rose lovely!'—but he was scorned by all men and by women too. For the women didn't want any help.

While they were well they did it all, and when they were ill some other woman came and did it. Simple jobs like dish-washing, bed-making and elementary cookery seemed beyond men who built the great ships for which the river was famous.

Of course, such things were not really beyond them. My father had been a soldier, and he could have looked after us as well then as I could look after my family now. He once made excellent bread after some argument with my mother, but it would have been more than her life was worth to tell anyone.

I don't want to give the impression that my father was like Andy Capp—a worthless, lazy, unchivalrous, self-indulgent egoist—but it is a coincidence that Andy's creator comes from our part of the country. Take all our fathers' good qualities away and you are left with something like that—the easy assumption of superiority, the rigid division of work and interests into what is suitable for a man and for a woman, and that touch of male ruthlessness and deliberate lack of imagination that prevented them from feeling how hard, dreary and unending so much of housekeeping and bringing up a family is. This was apparent on Sunday morning, Father's great day of rest. He rose late, breakfasted heavily, and scanned three Sunday papers. Meanwhile Mother, back from early church, was shoving great blocks of wood under the oven in preparation for the baking that took up half her day.

When the kitchen throbbed with heat and power like an engine room, he rose up and said, 'By, you've got this room like a furnace, hinney!' and went for a walk resplendent in his 'good' clothes—navy suit, hard hat, and carnation buttonhole. He did sometimes take us with him, which was, I suppose, a help in a way, but Mother had been lacing and brushing and buttoning us while he tutted over Saturday's sport.

We came back promptly at twelve to the gargantuan Sunday roast. Then we went to Sunday school and Father slept. If the kitchen table wasn't covered with the red-fringed tablecoth and Mother hadn't her best blouse and gold chain on by four o'clock he was distinctly put out. After tea and church he took her for a walk quite often, and made gentle fun of her inability to go as far as he would have liked.

A year or two ago when I was once more in the north I went to see an old couple now in their eighties. There was no new-fangled equality there. The old man sat serenely reading his sporting paper. His wife, a shadow of the vigorous woman of my childhood, still crept round him in a sort of parody of her former bustling efficiency. Sixty years of bland unhelpfulness were eloquent in every puff of his glowing pipe.

In an unguarded moment I mentioned making chocolate buns. I often used to when the children were small and my wife was tired. The effect was like dropping a bomb. An expression of incredulous contempt swept over the old lady's usually mild and kindly features.

'Chocolate buns! Ye never!' she exploded.

I had to pretend I'd been joking, but I felt they only half believed me and that I'd lost all claim to be a man.

Another feature of life in my childhood, and one which had immense social implications, was the 'room'. It was an invisible distinction because nearly all the streets of our town were alike in spite of the fact that they had different names. They were mostly arranged in hundred-yard-long blocks. The doorways were two and two with a bedroom in between. If you sat on the sill, as we often did waiting for a turn at bays or multikitty, you could sometimes hear through glass and lace curtain some night-shift trimmer or keelman snoring. The left-hand door of each pair led to a three-roomed downstairs house, the right-hand door to an upstairs one with four rooms. There were streets where houses had both up and downstairs, and even little four by two gardens, but they were the exceptions. The other sort depressingly prevailed, but though they all looked alike there was this great if invisible distinction—you either did or did not possess a 'room'.

I don't mean a kitchen, a bedroom of a scullery—we all had those—but a sitting room. A parlour, my South Country mother would call it; a front room, some people said, though it might often be at the back. But to most of us Tynesiders it was just 'the room'—an almost unused sanctuary that contained their best of everything.

Now obviously with small houses and big families, which were rather the rule when I was young, it was often difficult to have a 'room'. Some people frankly gave up the idea and entertained company from the ragman to the vicar in the kitchen, which I suspect the latter preferred. Others went to heroic lengths.

I have seen bedrooms that seemed one vast bed, so close were they together, and kitchens that became dormitories every night. Children slept in passages and even in cupboards. Strong men slung hammocks, and one's bedmates wouldn't always have satisfied the tables of kindred and affinity in the Prayer Book. Grandmothers tended to be tucked in anywhere. So did babies. And all this voluntary glad overcrowding, this warm willing cramped night-life, was in honour of the 'room'.

What was it like? As children we hardly knew. There were dire penalties for entering it at forbidden times.

'Ma, wor Jimmy's in the room and he's gor his working boots on!' brought swift and certain retribution.

The door was always kept shut—even locked in some houses, except on special occasions. For those it was always ready; clean to the Nth degree, the blind drawn, the light dim and religious, smelling of polish and wash-leather and upholstery. On the hearth the fire-irons and the ornamental men reining back their prancing horses gleamed through the chinks of last week's *North Mail* that covered them. The three-piece suite (you had to have one) was soft and elegant and cold. On the wall between wedding photographs and family groups and the twin lithographs of 'Accepted' and 'Rejected' the roses and grapes of a robustly horticultural wallpaper dominated where they got the chance.

Against one wall in the posher sort of room stood the piano—bought in the First World War. Its dark wood flashed like a mirror. Its candle brackets gleamed like the Crown Jewels. To this sublime instrument crept every evening the favoured musical one of the family, suitably washed and chastened, to disturb the almost audible silence with 'The Robin's Return'.

Some visitors were always entertained comfortably in the kitchen—'back-door company', as we say—but the room was the only place good enough for the vicar or the teacher or friends of a higher social level from the posh roads and avenues beyond the park. Then up went the

Venetian blind and off came the newspapers from the hearth. Off too came a mother's apron, and on if there was time went her silk blouse and gold chain. It was the best china that afternoon, and thin bread and butter and not a drop spilled or a crumb scattered.

Some people used their rooms every Sunday. Fathers would sleep there covered with the *News of the World* while the children were at Sunday school, and in the evening both parents might sit one on each side of the aspidistra commenting on the passing show in the street outside. One heard the tart 'There's Mrs. Robson going to St. John's. It's a wonder the roof doesn't fall on her.'

Or at the sight of a gaily-painted lady of uncertain virtue the long-drawn 'By . . .' that spoke volumes.

I liked the 'room' best at Christmas when a leaping coal fire transformed it, and the piano stood open all day with vases of holly on top. The 'mistletoe', as we called a bauble-decorated series of hoops, turned slowly in the draught at the window, and the paper chains hung from wall to wall. Exciting smells of Christmas cake and ginger wine chased away the Puritan odours of mere cleanliness for one blessed week.

It was a sad day when fathers took the decorations down and mothers locked the piano, and the Japanese screen was back in front of the grate where we had sprawled and laughed and roasted our chestnuts. There mightn't be another fire in the 'room' for another twelve-month unless someone in the family happened to be courting. Then it came into its own again. Mothers would transfer half the kitchen fire on a shovel in spite of a father's 'Why should I starve for wor Annie?' and light the gas at half-cock before they came in.

'I've put a bit of fire for you in the room, hinneys,' she'd say indulgently and that was the last we'd see of the lovers.

Sunday, Christmas, love—death too, for it was in the 'room' that our dead lay in pathetic state amongst the candles and flowers. The sweet suffocating smell of lilies mingled with the sharper tang of sherry given to the cabmen and the bearers. It was a long mile to the hillside cemetery against a bleak sea-wind.

When they'd gone the 'room' fire would be lighted, and the dreadful empty space where the coffin had stood filled up with friendly furniture again, and preparations made for the sad ritual meal an hour or two later.

I remember the muted conversations of such occasions, the sudden bursts of hilarity that only emphasised our sorrow, and the guilt for enjoying the rare taste of ham sandwiches which seldom came our way at any other time.

'The room' isn't such a holy of holies nowadays, I'm told. The young have invaded it with their record-players and transistors. Polished fire-irons are a thing of the past, and the piano stands, not unpolished, but unplayed. 'Accepted' and 'Rejected' went to the jumble sale years ago.

But when I knocked at the front door a summer ago, where many years past I was 'back-door company', the door was opened cautiously and my greeting was 'Come in, hinney, Thank God its only you. Wor Jane Anne was married yesterday and the room's a tip!'

Of course, it wasn't. It was immaculate.

Another institution in my youth was the mantelpiece. We still have them, of course, but I don't suppose there's much on yours, and there certainly isn't much on mine. It isn't even a real mantelpiece—just the top part of a modern grate. There's about a yard of narrow ledge and two or three steps from which I'm always knocking small ornaments of fortunately no value. On the ledge there's a rather nice china donkey, a stamp-box that was once my mother's, a pebble from Holy Island, half a dozen of my wife's ubiquitous hair-grips, and a postcard from some lucky friends enjoying a holiday abroad. Not even a clock—it's not wide enough.

Now at home we had a real mantelpiece. It was a thick wide shelf high above the kitchen grate. From it hung a piece of velvet drapery festooned with bobbles, and below it there was a hollow brass rail, perhaps for drying clothes. Ours was kept dazzlingly bright but never used. By standing on my mother's nursing chair I could, by putting my lips to one end of this rod, blow a note like that of a Swiss mountaineer calling up his cattle. I often did so, especially when my father was asleep in the back room after night shift in the steelworks, and it never failed to wake him.

The surface of our mantelpiece was crowded with things. Everyone's was. I suppose it was partly because there wasn't anywhere else to put the daily debris of living. People had less furniture then. In our kitchen there was a big table, a number of nondescript chairs, a bookcase (the only one in the street) and an old leather sofa that opened up to make an extremely uncomfortable bed. There was a cupboard, and a set of fixed shelves that were part of the house.

We kept food in the cupboard and crockery on the shelves. The table was always either laid for a meal, or in use for ironing, or set out with my brother's clockwork train, or doing duty as a workbench for my father to mend our shoes.

There was really only the mantelpiece to keep things on, so no wonder it was overcrowded. In the middle was the clock, a kind of toy grandfather one, made in Guildford in 1780. It had a cross face—or did I just think so because once when I was playing with the fire it fell on my head? My mother, a simple soul, saw it as the hand of God saving me from certain conflagration, but I disliked that clock for ever afterwards, and had no compunction about selling it for half a crown when we broke our home up in the thirties.

On either side of the clock were two boots, green ones made of china. They contained a multiplicity of objects, screws, stamps, sealing wax, needles, thimbles, a magnet, a Swiss crucifix, a lucky bean from South Africa studded with small worthless diamonds, marbles, several unidentifiable keys, and a small reindeer made of white bone. There were lots of other things too, but I've forgotten them.

'Look in the boot, hinney!' my father would say if any small object was missing, and crash! the left boot would be emptied on to whatever fraction of the table was available, to be followed inevitably by the right. Nothing was ever in the first boot.

Next to the boots the symmetry of the mantelpiece varied a little. On one side there was a sea-shell, on the other the tea-caddy. I remember the sea-shell; its back was like a tortoise, and I would put it to my ear and listen to the murmur of the sea. Sometimes in the thirties when I was out of work and listless with despair I'd stand for ages with it to my ear and be comforted by the grave assurance of breaking waves.

The tea-caddy was covered with pictures of English royalties—the old Queen, of course, and Edward and Alexander, and a youthful George and Mary who were crowned the day I was born. Indeed, next to the shell was a mug commemorating the occasion. The symmetry was restored by our two beakers celebrating the Treaty of Versailles, 'peace pots', as we called them, and continued by a pair of vases of bloated proportions and revolting colours. Round one a lion was pursued by Zulus. On the other stags bounded across what my mother claimed to be the Cairngorm Mountains. Sometimes there were flowers in these vases, but more often they contained our few documents, the rent book, my grandmother's will, birth certificates, and my mother's marriage lines, ready I suppose for the remote possibility of their being questioned!

This doesn't leave much mantelpiece, and indeed the things on the end often dropped off on to the heads of whoever happened to be sitting on the chairs at each side of the fireplace.

Fortunately there were usually only letters leaning precariously against the vase at one side, and bills at the other. I read all the letters as soon as I could understand grown-up handwriting, standing on the steel fender with one foot on the black horse that reared up on the oven side from the rubby-stoned hearth.

I remember the long one that brought news of my scholarship to the grammar school, the square black-edged one that said that my grandfather was dead down in far-off Surrey, merry ones from my mother's friends in the servants' hall, full of society gossip, and the aristocratic envelope that every birthday until the end of his life brought a fiver from her old master.

The crises of life centred on our mantelpieces, so that, as I have described elsewhere in this book, when I brought Fred's down in ruins I felt guilty of the destruction of their private lives. Fred's parents were out at the time, but when I saw his big sister's stricken face, and heard her whispered, 'You'd better go home, son,' I crept out feeling like a murderer.

I'm rather glad my modern fireplace bears so little relation to the ones at home. Even though it must be getting on for half a century since I brought that old-fashioned mantelpiece down I don't think I could face one again without feeling as I did that fatal afternoon that I had brought somebody's world to an end.

On the Corner and Down the Dene

In the late twenties the lanes between streets were paved instead of being cobbled. This made football easier, and their narrow friendliness was more exciting than the wider front streets where irate housewives objected to feet scuffling over rubby-stoned semi-circles of pavement, and traffic—still fifty per cent horse-drawn—was a constant nuisance.

Besides, nearly everyone used the back door, which was reached via a wooden gate in a high brick wall. If you called for a friend by banging with the polished front-door knocker (taking care to keep off the spotless step) a sarcastic 'Front-door company!' made you realise that you didn't rank with the doctor, the vicar, or the rent man, and after that you walked round the block and hammered on the back gate, which no one ever seemed to mind.

When you made a new friend in some other part of our small town you played (until your friendship cooled) at his 'Corner', as we called it, which meant his street and back lane. Later you returned to your own, and took your accustomed place as leader or follower there as if you had never been away.

I remember that when Wesley was my best friend, I spent all my free time in the lane between Leopold Street, where he lived, and Caroline Street, which was back to back with it.

Lanes are decently wide in the north-east, at least compared with those I was to see in Lancashire years later, mere alleys where two people could scarcely pass, and Yorkshire, where they had economised in space so much that many streets had no lanes at all, nor even back doors.

Our lanes were adequate, about fifteen feet wide, and as these streets named after foreign royalties were only eighty yards long, they were always full of people. Chiefly children, of course. Little girls played bays and stotted balls; football was perennial except for a few hot months when we turned to cricket, and grown-ups crossed from yard to yard visiting one another's houses.

They were a mixed lot—no more mixed, I suppose, than those in my street at the other end of the town, where the streets were called after admirals and generals (not that we ever knew), but being a stranger at someone else's corner made me, I suppose, more than usually observant.

Wesley's mother was called Zibbah, which would be odd now, but biblical names were much commoner then, and so was the custom of giving a surname for a Christian one. Wesley was an obvious but quite unremarkable example. Her two sisters, Esther and Rachel, lived opposite in Caroline Street, which in the invisible, and to me baseless, hierarchy of streets, was rather better than Leopold where 'poor Zibbah' lived.

If a little woman in a grubby pinny, arms folded over flat chest, scuttled across the lane it would be Esther. She apologised for living, and had the maddening habit of finishing all your sentences for you. Her husband was a large pompous man who never hurried. We put this down to his job. Somewhere on the outskirts of the town the council were making a new road that would eventually be opened by the Queen Mother, then Duchess of York, and Uncle Bob's job was to walk in front of the steam-roller with a fine big red flag. I can't think why unless they'd never heard of the repeal of the Act that had once made this necessary, but even allowing for Northumberland being the last county in England you'd have thought it would have been proclaimed there by 1925.

In his off hours he liked to listen to oratorios on his antique gramophone—'But who may abide', and things like that—and though he never went to church, he had a strong moral sense. When one of Wesley's many cousins bought a pop record—we had such things then, of course, Leyton and Johnson, the Savoy Orpheans, Gracie Fields, Rudy Vallee and such stars of yesteryear—he heard it once through: and then taking it with the silent calm of extreme rage to the window, he flung it into the back-yard, where, records being brittle then, it shivered into a hundred black pieces. A twangy American voice had just sung,

'She's got two pretty legs with dimpled knees,
A pair of arms and they know how to squeeze,
A perfect mouth (and I'm hard to please)
But everybody does it in Hawaii!'

Fortunately, Uncle Bob never lived to see the permissive society. Wesley's other aunt, Rachel, was as buxom and confident as Esther was mild and diffident. Her children did well and the rest of the family were made to feel it. One boy was an engineer 'with letters after his name', one taught music, if only at a shilling a lesson, and married the

Rialto Cinema violinist, and even the youngest, Warwick, enjoyed the distinction of being mildly delicate, and was able to luxuriate in bed while the rest of us ran down the streets in the seven o'clock morning to our jobs in the shipyard, catching hot rivets on the windy upper deck, or marking out cold steel plates with a surly mate who sometimes didn't speak all day except to give orders. Rachel would stand with her ample behind to Zibbah's fire, her skirts lifted regardless of us boys, with no more excuse than 'By, it's cold this morning. My hint end's like ice!'

Her husband Uncle Ebbie was a tall thin man with a grey-streaked red beard, rather like pictures I had seen of G.B.S. He had sailed before the mast as a boy, and perhaps the privations of those last grim voyages round the Horn had preyed on his mind. At any rate in his backyard he had a small shed, and in it he saved all the kinds of things people usually throw away: odd nuts and bolts, pieces of string, paper bags, cocoa tins, jam-jars, keys, wheels, derelict watches, broken gilt picture frames—you couldn't mention anything of that sort that wasn't somewhere on Ebbie's neatly shelfed shed. But to absolutely no purpose. Ask him if he had, say, a pair of old push-chair wheels, much in demand in springtime for making bogies, and a delighted smile would crease his weather-beaten face.

'Aye, I've got just the thing; ball-bearings and all!'

Ask him for it, if you dared, and his expression would change from pleasure to a kind of nervous fear.

'But I might need it, hinney. You always never know.'

Uncle Ebbie's backyard was as you would expect, as neat and clean as his shed. Not so Ronny Baxter's next door. Ronny was a young dock labourer a few years older than Wesley and me. His hobbies included hen-keeping, carpentry, and health and strength. He was devoted to a paper of that name which was full of photographs of hideously overdeveloped men grasping dumb-bells. One of his many misconceptions was that cold water was a great toughener, and I remember bitter winter days when Wesley and I poured bucket after bucket of freezing water from the yard tap over a naked Ronny, roaring with his simpleton's laughter while White Leghorns and Plymouth Rocks scurried to the safety of the wood-pile, and small girls collected round the open back gate to watch the fun.

Once this uproar proved too much for Ronny's father, a *malade imaginaire* whom we hadn't seen for over three years. An emaciated figure in a long night-shirt and slippers emerged waving a volume of the *Encyclopaedia Britannica* (through which he was working) and we fled down the lane pursued by this harmless incoherent apparition.

The next time I saw him, his second and last exodus from the bedroom that had become his refuge, he cut a very different figure. Dressed in frock-coat, top-hat, and spats, and wearing the red rosette of his party, he tottered on a silver-mounted stick to the Methodist chapel schoolroom in Charlotte Street to record his vote—against Ramsay MacDonald, I suppose.

Three odd denizens of the lane were Pat, Kevin and Leo Macnally. They lived with a haggard elder sister whose lips were always moving—in prayer, I suppose now, though then I thought her a trifle mad. They were very poor and worked the local dumps for coal long before the bad days when we all did. They sold their pathetic sacks of 'small' from door to door. Imelda Macnally roved the countryside, which was hardly country at all, armed with an old axe, and brought back stolen fencing and portions of hawthorn hedge which she bundled up and threw into people's backyards without ceremony. It was customary to throw a copper or two back with nothing said on either side.

Of course, they were Catholics, and their local church, known to us Protestants as 'the black hole', had the usual three or four masses on a Sunday morning. Being so poor, they had only one decent blue serge suit and white silk muffler, our badge of respectability, and each youth would go to a different service so that they could all wear, in turn, the same suit. Then on Monday Imelda would pawn it to get the rent and redeem it on the following Saturday.

Pat and Kevin sometimes worked on the roads, though in a much humbler capacity than Uncle Bob with his red flag, but poor Leo was simple—even simpler than Ronny—and played with us though he must have been a good five years older. We played at the bottom of the lane and the girls at the top, except in winter, when we all drew together round the one quivering gas lamp that lit up the gable end with its advertisement for Truman's Ales and a poster denouncing the Zinoviev letter. Maudie Garde would be there and Harriet Dodds and all the Branders, six handsome little Irish girls with jet-black hair, and, queen of the lot, Marion Miller in her red boots who organised the kissing games that involved so much running and such a rich reward.

In the summer, however, we got tired of the corner and would often go to Monkton Dene, especially in the evening, to light fires, which I enjoyed, and observe 'nature' as our schoolmasters had taught us to do, but chiefly to jump the stream that ran down the middle of the dene, a practice which I dreaded but could not avoid.

The fact is I was an arrant coward, afraid of big dogs, not daring to go on the high 'figure of eight' motor ride at South Shields, and extremely unlikely to try to stop a runaway horse.

The stream was neither very wide nor very deep, but a certain amount of nerve is needed to launch out across open water, and this I seemed to lack. I always jumped last, made several run-ups and invariably ended wet to the waist. We made our way from the footbridge at the top of the dene where the waterfall droned on the pebble shore down to a fearful jump we had christened 'Hawthorn Leap'.

I wasn't the only one who couldn't attempt this one, but to sail over the small may bush that blocked your view and drop (was it only four or five feet?) on to the muddy foreshore of the stream was one of my private daydreams through many a dull school lesson. I never expected to be able to do it. Trailing after the others, wet-footed and breathless, I managed in time to do every other jump in some way or other, but at Hawthorn Leap I stood aside and left it to the older lads of Wesley's corner, admiring but not daring to emulate their unimaginative courage.

Mooning about at home one rainy Sunday I found a gold-bladed ornamental paper-knife. I didn't know what it was and stuck it in my cricket belt to show my mother.

'It's a paper-knife—for opening letters or cutting pages in a new book,' she said.

I must have looked disappointed at its unmilitary use,

for she added, 'It belonged to young Lord Rowland. He got the M.C. taking his battery over the Modder River.'

My mother was always talking about the Boer War and the brave deeds young men whose parents she had been in service with had done in it. That night I suggested going up the dene to jump. The boys took some persuading because it had been raining for days and the take-offs would all be slippery, but eventually we started out. I had screwed my courage to the sticking place, was determined to excel at every jump, and to try Hawthorn Leap for the first time. Under my shorts I could feel Lord Rowland's knife against my left thigh and was game for anything.

The feeling didn't last. The stream in the dene was inches wider, running with an ominous note and full of debris from higher up. It swirled along, opaque and glassy green. Half-heartedly we started off on our ritual score of jumps. Long before the final test we were very wet, but had gained in determination, and for once I had kept well up and wasn't jumping last. Even Bob Forest remarked approvingly, 'You're improving, Barty. We'll make a man of you yet!'

At last we reached the fatal spot. Bob inspected the take-off. He shook a connoisseur's head. 'Ower muddy the night, lads. We'll have to give it a miss.'

Everyone turned obediently away. I put my hand under my jersey and felt the trusty paper-knife. I remembered Lord Rowland and a river in Africa somewhat wider than this North Country burn.

'I'll do it!' I shouted in a voice I hardly recognised as my own. The dene rang with their good-natured jeers.

'I'll do it!' I shouted again, though with considerably less conviction. But it was too late to draw back; they were gathering round to see me make a fool of myself as usual.

I did the run-up once, twice, and again laughter filled the dene. The third time I knew I was going. Some feet other than mine were using my sodden shoes. I reached the glittering rain-soaked bush and launched out into space.

Down, down I went, feeling like an airman before his 'chute opens. I had a confused glimpse of rushing water full of twigs and fallen blossom. Then I hit the opposite bank and a concealed stone in the thick mud. My ankle was badly sprained and my short-lived courage did not long survive the keen pain, but Bob and Wesley and the others helped me back to my own corner and very decently turned a blind eye to my inevitable tears. They even called the jump 'Barton's Leap' for a week or two until my natural cowardice returned, and I failed to jump it in dry weather when the stream wasn't half as wide.

Well, the dene's a park now—made by the unemployed sometime in the thirties—and quite recently they've pulled down Leopold Street and Caroline Street, and the chapel and the old lamp and the corner where we played are all buried under the great road that the traffic pours along to go under the Tyne through the tunnel that the 'canny bairn', as we called the Duchess of York's elder daughter—now our gracious queen—opened a few months ago.

And all the people I knew at Wesley's corner are either dead or dispersed, but what ghosts must haunt that empty stretch of tarmac with its string of neon lights on summer dusks and winter nights, what ghosts!

A Trip to the Well

I ALWAYS liked Monday, in spite of its back-to-school smell of ink and sore knuckles for being slow at mental arithmetic because it was washing day, and when I came home there'd be clothes strung across the kitchen in all directions. They were as gay as bunting, and if my mother was only a distant figure in a linenly mist, and you couldn't read the paper by the diminished light of the gas mantle, and my father fled to the nearest cinema as soon as he'd had his tea, what did it matter?

It was different, like spring-cleaning, when chairs were piled on top of one another and we had dinner off the bedroom wash-stand with yesterday's *North Mail* for a cloth. I loved change, and when after my father was ill the fire was lighted in the big bedroom and I could read *White Fang* in the basket chair (as long as I didn't make it creak) I'm afraid I hoped he'd stay ill (painlessly, of course) for a long time. This love of change was just as true for out of doors as well as in. Nothing was so depressing as a long wet day when the front doors were all shut and rain stotted off the cobbles, and no one had said, 'Howway, play in wor passage.'

But things were seldom so depressingly without incident for long. A street-singer sidled up the gutter uttering his series of mournful cries that never seemed to add up to a song, or Mr. Sanderson's Belsize conked out and we had to push it along to his garage, or the yellow fever van came to take some luckless child away to the isolation hospital—a bare grey building ominously close to the cemetery.

We sought and loved diversion, and the longer the diversion lasted, the better. Once—I suppose it was in the mid-twenties—the whole town changed from middens to water-closets. Every back lane was seamed with trenches where the new drain-pipes were to be laid and on long summer evenings we re-enacted the great battles of the First World War, sometimes repelling balls of well-aimed clay with the very tin hats that our fathers had worn through the horrors of Loos and the Somme.

The best thing of all was a watchy's fire, especially in early autumn when the darkening evenings were just cold enough to make us grateful for its acrid warmth, and Orion and the Hunter's moon hung over the mysterious turnip fields that stretched between us and Bede's Well, and the great bulk of the slag-heap.

Somehow they always put the little hut and the glowing brazier of coke on the open bit of field no one had built on yet at the top of Grenville Street. The wind leapt like a sword across pit cottages and the golf-course and down the north and south-running streets from the river, where crane lights got mixed up with the stars, and a muted clang and roar that would have startled strangers went as unnoticed by us as main road traffic does to the children of today.

The limping Irishman who had erected his diminutive den of timber, sacking, and corrugated iron, with its back to the north wind, would be sitting on his plank seat puffing at a clay pipe.

From my front door halfway down the street I would see the outline of his shelter in the gathering dusk, and the ever brightening glow of his fire, and homework done or not done, I would run (as I shall never be able to do again) up the couple of hundred yards of pavement to this Mecca with an excited happiness few circumstances have given me as intensely since. Some of this was the mere exuberance of youth—that state of physical perfection when you feel you could run on and on for ever. The late September evening air, the faint bitter scent of some chrysanthemums on one of the allotments, and, as I joined the gang ranged around the brazier, the coke fumes and hot metal all contributed to it. But best of all, and giving my heart that sharp stab of delightful pain I knew so well then, was the fact that Laura was there.

She was a fair girl, straight-haired and straight-nosed, with that blue-eyed Viking look quite common in the north. And why not? The Vikings had sailed their dreaded ships up the Tyne and up its once clear little tributary, the Don, time and again hundreds of years ago. In fact, they'd burned down Bede's monastery that stood on the eastern edge of our town at least twice. Surely some of them had settled down in the Durham and Northumberland villages alongside the English, and even now the type kept reappearing. Laura was an example, and we boys all adored her. It wasn't the same if she wasn't playing out. Winnie was nice and affectionate and always good for a quick kiss in any running game. Stella was spoiled and spoke to some people and not others. Her father was a foreman plater and they were (by our standards) rolling in money. Elsie was plain and friendly and though everybody liked her, no one ever fell for her. The Watson girls were poor and shabby. Their father drank and by a curious irony their mother, an ardent Rechabite, scrubbed out the Golden Fleece and the Rising Sun to eke out their slender means. There were others too, Olive and Jenny, and little loquacious Agnes, but no one to touch Laura. And as far as I knew no one had touched her. Not that she was a snob like Stella. She spoke to everybody, but rather as a queen might—as though no one boy mattered more than another. And that was a good thing, because I wasn't handsome like Robert Hall or a good footballer like Rinso Selby, or even brave like Jim Walker who could do the hardest jump in Monkton Dene—a dreadful drop of about five feet with a hawthorn bush to clear first, and a stony landing on the far side of the stream.

Laura seemed no more impressed by one sort of boy than another. None had caused her an instant's heart-ache yet, and though we all regretted it, at least it kept us equal in our united (and of course untold) devotion, and free from jealousy. You'd have thought kissing games which always began on dark September evenings and went on until real winter drove us off the streets would give us some clue, but the truth was that though we all boasted that we'd caught her in some back lane off Grenville or Anson Street, no one ever had.

There she was, however, cool and friendly as ever, with a word for me (which was more than Stella had) as soon as I joined the circle standing back from the red-hot brazier like an innocuous wolf-pack from a trapper's fire.

'Done your Virgil, Barty ?'—we were in the same form at grammar school.

'Not yet,' I said, meaning to wrestle with it later by the light of a red shipyard candle in my bedroom.

'It's a funny bit about Galatea pelting a chap with apples and running behind the trees. "Salices" means "Willows".'

'Like "Down by the sally gardens", mebbe?'

'Never thought of that. What a clever boy!'

'What'll we play tonight?' asked Jim, a bit truculent at all this learned conversation. He was still at elementary school and regarded me with my French and Latin and satchel and spectacles as a bit of a freak. Moreover, he knew I couldn't do half the big jumps in Monkton Dene and had the naturally brave boy's genial contempt for the coward.

'Catchee Kissee!' cried Winnie immediately, who was evidently in an affectionate mood.

'Leavo,' said Robert Hall shortly, and, as he was our natural leader, 'Leavo' it had to be. For the next half-hour we ran and yelled and caught one another, filled the bases (chalked circles round the lamps) and emptied them again with one of Rinso's daring dummy-selling runs like a rugger three-quarter and the welcome cry of 'Leavo'.

To catch a boy, you grabbed him and spat over his head, but a rare delicacy made us content to merely touch a girl without this extra and often ill-aimed sign of conquest. Meanwhile Martin, the watchy, sat puffing contentedly at his pipe and reading a battered little book. He seemed as immune to the heat as if his shabby clothes had been made of asbestos, and one by one as we got tired we came and sat on the hot cobbles, watching the shimmering patterns the smoke made above the brazier, and snuffing its rather choky smell with great satisfaction.

'What are you reading, Mr. Brady?' asked Laura politely.

' 'Tis me Missal, child; what you would call a prayer book.'

She put out a unconsciously imperious hand for it, and turned a page or two by the light of the fire.

' "*Domine non sum dignus*"—"Lord I am not good enough" ? Why, the English is on the other side of the page. Don't you know Latin, Mr. Brady?'

'Not much, miss. You see when I was your age I was a drummer boy in the Army. I hadn't the schooling.'

'I thought all you Catholics knew Latin,' said Jim Walker scornfully. His people were keen Methodists and he always had to spout a piece full of 'verilys' and 'selahs' at anniversary services.

'They all know a bit,' said Martin, 'though there's not many are the great scholars St. Bede was.'

'You mean our Venerable Bede?' asked Robert in a voice that showed he claimed our local saint as a respectable Anglican. We all looked across the rough grass where we played football and the dark fields beyond full of turnips and corn-stubble to where, about a mile away, a spring (known locally as Bede's Well) bubbled up under the slag-heap.

There was a silly and inevitable rumour that a dark passage ran from somewhere near it right under the slag-heap and the colliery railway and the park and half the town, and emerged at the old church where the ruins of the monastery were. There Bede had lived man and boy when our town was a simple Saxon settlement in the green hawthorny country south of the Tyne.

Of course, such a passage didn't exist, though we often

tried to find the entrance—in daylight, of course. Nevertheless, the spring was there and you sometimes found an old Irishman kneeling by it muttering his prayers, or a woman crossing herself as she passed the bubbling brown basin that fed a stream which trickled across the golf-course where pit-men exercised their whippets.

Tonight a light mist was rising over the fields and soon the Hunter's moon would rise above it. A menacing bellow came now and then from the darkness. The farmer had turned a herd of bullocks on to the stubble field beyond which the well lay. Martin put away his prayer book and took out an odd flat bottle.

'While I'm lighting me lamps,' he said, 'I wonder if one of yous would slip over to yon well and fill this up with holy water?'

Slip over? More than a mile across the misty fields stiff with fierce invisible cattle to fumble in the well under the black volcanic bulk of the slag-heap!

'What do you want it for?' asked Robert.

'One of me childer is sick,' answered Martin simply.

'And what good will yon well water do it?' retorted Jim Walker. 'Ye might as well fill it from the park pond.'

'Or your scullery tap,' said Stella, 'if you've got one.'

'Oh, we have one, miss,' said Martin simply, limping off to light his dozen or so red oil lamps, 'but 'twoudn't be the same at all.'

'For shame, Stella Russell,' said good-natured Elsie, and went to help Martin. So did Jim and Robert. Stella flounced in to do her piano practice, and the others sat on in a sleepy daze, overcome by the drifting fumes of the fire.

Martin and his helpers dumped the warning lamps along the open trench the navvies had made. The little whisky bottle stood on the plank seat near his newspaper and blue bait can. Laura and I hovered round it. In a moment one of us would have to pluck up courage to take it and go. Evidently no one else would. A particularly loud bellow came from the cornfield. I shuddered, but I couldn't let Laura beat me and forfeit my chances with her for ever. I stepped into the shelter across the blast of heat, slipped the small flat bottle into my blazer pocket and set off.

'Don't be too long, Barty,' said Laura, her long hair streaming on the rising wind. 'I've got my maths to do.'

So she was going to wait and see if I dared do it. I had thought for a moment we could go together, but no such luck, though she did wave as I looked back from the edge of the turnip field to the beloved Viking figure outlined against the watchy's fire. The first field took a long time to cross. This was partly because of the irregularities caused by the turnips being half out of the ground, and partly because of the knee-high mist that made them invisible; but mostly because the next field was where the bullocks stalked among the stubble. But all too soon I was at the fence that divided nervous safety from what I thought of as real danger. I was strongly tempted to work my way along this fence to a narrow path that ran from the farmhouse down to Bede's Well. It had a low stone wall on both sides and there would have been company too—pairs of lovers locked in their tranced embraces. 'What do they *do*, Barty?' Winnie had once asked me when we were coming home that way from Monkton Dene. She was all for kissing, but after five minutes she got bored and felt in her pockets for a bull's-eye or a glacier mint.

But I knew that Laura expected me to go the field way, so I slowly climbed the fence, cold and rimy to my sweating hands, and advanced cautiously over the couple of hundred yards of stubble that separated me from the well. I could hear it bubbling faintly in the intervals of the wind. Above was a clear sky full of stars, ahead the comforting puffing of the slag-engine making its slow ascent of the miniature mountain. Far away there was the confused babble of voices like a distant schoolyard at break. These were all the children of Durham and Northumberland who were still playing out in the riverside streets, and, under it all, the bass of our orchestra, the night-shift noises of steelworks and shipyards. Immediately ahead of me, however, were the tearing sounds of cattle cropping the stubble, and their black bulks to right and left of me, legless above the chilly mist.

One or two of them lifted inquiring heads, but when they were lowered again it was not to charge me but to go on eating. My heart stopped hammering. This was easier than I thought. Then suddenly my foot caught in something and I fell forward. My outstretched hands sunk into a living body hairy and warm, a huge object that sprang up with an unearthly roar flinging me on my back, and galloped away. Immediately the field was full of the thunder of hoofs, as the herd, frightened by the panic of the bullock I'd tripped over, raced round in circles while I lay sobbing until they'd quietened down again.

Stumbling to my feet, I found I was only a few yards from the far fence. Thankfully I clambered over it, ran down to the eerie-sounding well and filled Martin's bottle. An owl flew out of a crevice in the slag-heap wall and drifted silent as a leaf over the golf course. I stood by the well till I'd calmed down again.

Did honour demand that I re-cross the cornfield once more? I suppose it did, but I compromised by going along by the wall up to the turnip-field boundary and then across that. At the edge of the field Laura was waiting. She actually took my cold wet hand in her warm one and we walked slowly back.

'You survived the bulls then?' she asked.

'I fell head first over one lying down. Thought me last moment had come!'

She laughed a lot, but kindly, not like Stella Russell would have done. The wind blew her long hair across my face. Above us the stars glittered, Orion, the Chair, our beloved Plough, and the Pole star high above Northumberland.

'I must go in now and do my maths,' said Laura as we approached the fire. 'They've all gone in.' Then irrelevantly, 'Robert Hall asked me to go to the pictures with him on Saturday.'

'Hope you like it,' I said lamely.

'I'm not going,' she said scornfully. 'He wouldn't have done what you did for Mr. Brady. I think you're much nicer.'

She gave my hand a quick squeeze and was off like a deer down Anson Street.

'Queen and huntress chaste and fair', I thought, but I'd write a better poem about her than that tonight in my candle-lit bedroom.

Martin was drinking strong sweet tea from his can lid when I gave him the bottle of cloudy well-water. He made a quick sign of the cross over it and put it carefully in his pocket. Then he rinsed the chipped enamel lid out, refilled it and handed it to me. I stood there drinking tea and munching a corned-beef sandwich, watching the red lamps flickering down the length of the street.

'Ta, son,' said Martin with his gentle politeness. 'Ye see I can't leave me fire in case the polis comes round, and begob I couldn't run across them fields like you now.'

'What made you lame?' I asked.

'The war son. I was a trooper in the Skins.'

'The Skins?'

'The Inneskillen Dragoon Guards. A Jerry lancer got me through the knee in October '14. That's why I'm a watchy. Ye'd better go in now son, it's getting late.'

He sighed and turned back to the fire. I thought of the long lonely hours ahead of him.

'Come and keep us company tomorrow night. And don't think what you done'll be forgotten. She'll reward ye.'

She? What did he know about Laura, the renewed thought of whom made my heart sing as I walked down the empty street to my familiar door. I thought in my innocence that he must have guessed, but the pronoun meant quite different persons to a fourteen-year-old boy in love and a pious Irish watchy, though it was to be twenty years before I realised who he was referring to.

The Nighted Ferry

I NEVER walked down the long sloping street to the boat-landing in the dark (it was always dark—summer or winter when I made this compulsive circular tour) without Housman's lines repeating themselves again and again in my expectant mind:

> 'Crossing alone the nighted ferry,
> With the one coin for fee,
> Who on the banks of Lethe waiting,
> Count you to find? Not me.'

Only you needed two coins, because, unlike the classical dead, I was coming back, and a second 'nighted ferry' would bring me across the Tyne again to my own side an hour or so later and a couple of miles farther down the river.

The two coins were pennies, and twopence a trivial sum, but it was a penny world then. You got your 'Saturday penny' year after year from when you were big enough to pull yourself up to the level of our little house-shop windows, and there were wonderful sweets and toys to be bought with it. 'Down the street' there was Piper's Penny Bazaar, and at home a mysterious red metal box on the staircase wall into which a penny had to be dropped before the gas would hiss and burst into yellow light. And if the mantle was broken, as being fragile it often was, in some schoolboy horseplay, a penny candle was our only light for the rest of the evening. Later in my childhood, when we had changed to electricity, the meter took only shillings, and as that often meant a day's food, gentle candle-light was more common than the harsh glare of an unshaded bulb.

Perhaps that is why the sight of a single candle on a stand in church always reminds me of home (and you could buy a church candle for a penny until quite recently), while, oddly enough, so did the naked bulb dangling on its frayed flex from wartime barrack-room ceilings.

The 'nighted ferry' required twopence, unless you risked some foy boatman bringing you back from Northumberland to Durham in his sculler, and foy boatmen—who go out to ships coming up the river and execute commissions for incoming merchant seamen—were not to be relied on. Also when I was young I was afraid to be so near the deep green water with its smells of oil, paint, sewage and the sea, and when I was older and earning my pittance in a riverside office I could usually manage the fare at the expense of one of the paper packets of five Woodbines—hot and satisfying little cigarettes, the consumption of which was almost as necessary to me as food, and sometimes had to do instead.

I could, of course, have walked into the country. There were a few miles of open fields and hedges, sharp hawthorns through which a perpetual wind blew, and I sometimes did; but it wasn't the real country for which my mother's reminiscences had always made me heart-sick, and whenever I could afford it, I always sought the grimmest industrial scenery and the meanest streets. I only asked that they should not be those of my own small town with which I had the usual love-hate relationship, but somewhere different, strange, where streets had unfamiliar names at least, and no one I ever met there was known, or need be spoken to.

I nearly always made my tour alone. Sometimes if Fred or some other friend was particularly flush he would reluctantly waste twopence and come with me, and then we would have one of those long long conversations about life that I liked so much—conversations that ranged from comparative trivialities like speculations about Laura's or Isa's amatory preferences, to the existence of God. But such conversations usually took place round the lamp, or squatting hour after hour at our corner—the tiny oblong of extra pavement in front of the one real shop. There were several of us who were rather more articulate and better read than our shabby appearance would have suggested, and I sometimes thought that Socrates himself would not have declined to take his place against the sheltering wall of Mrs. Owen's two-by-four garden that smelled of cats as much as nasturtiums, and guide our juvenile intellectual exercises.

However, every now and then I left the claustrophobic security of Grenville Street, and, making sure I had my precious two coins, set out. I made for the upriver ferry, hurrying down too-well-known streets till I was through the turnstile and on the heaving deck of the boat, with the mysterious coloured lights of the river throwing their broken lances across to Wallsend, and gusts of oily warmth coming up from the engine room. Then the siren would screech, the screw begin to churn, a late passenger or two run up the gangway, and we were off on our five-minute voyage to Northumberland, another county, and the possibility of adventure.

Being away from my town, even if it was only by the width of the river, made it easier to think about my problems more clearly, and as I climbed the steep street on the other side, under the lee of the ballast hill, a sandy eminence which had no doubt supplied many a Tyne keel with its makeweight of sandy soil, I felt freer, and if not exactly light-hearted, at least less oppressed than I so often felt in the close confinement of home streets.

Here, when I was a schoolboy, I thought out my problems of home and family, resolved to be less obstinate and rebellious towards my sick and unemployed father, and, after his death, to be more patient with my good and simple, but exasperating mother. Here I fought, without much success, the crisis of puberty; put two and two together and very occasionally made four about birth and sex; sorted out my many and agonising loves, removed only by a river and a few streets from where they were reading, or doing their homework, or walking the long suburban road where everyone walked—but made smaller, less oppressive even by this small distance.

Did I really love Ethel? When we stood together at the corner of Clayton Street and I smelled her hair and the freshness of her school blouse and ached to take her into my inexperienced arms I thought so. Her shy smile, full of affection, and touched with anxiety in case her mother should come round the corner, made her very sweet. Her letters, long and literate in spite of our mutual lack of education, were passionate and touching. But did I really love her? Was I—sinful, proud, obstinate, and irresponsible—good enough to? And when I wasn't thinking about Ethel I thought of Daisy, my profane love. Daisy had a reputation. She was a tall brown-eyed girl who walked like a courtesan and behaved like one too, if it is possible to do so when most of the time you are working in a fruit shop and can be seen any day making precarious pyramids of Worcester Pearmains.

Daisy slapped my face for some quite inoffensive remark when we were all chatting in a group outside church one Sunday, but I knew, and she knew, and she knew I knew, that her gesture was only a token of interest, and when she loitered for me at the end of the street and smiled and murmured, 'I'm very sorry,' as I passed her on my way to the park, I thought that she was mine for the asking.

And after one of these self-exploratory walks I did ask her, and as we lay on the banks of Robber's Lonnin, a country lane leading to pit-village Boldon, she refused me what I'd heard she'd denied to few. 'Do my kisses prove unresponsive?' she asked (I suspected she read *Peg's Paper* and *The Red Letter* in the intervals of weighing out Jerseys and Jaffas), and later, 'No. You're a nice boy but you don't really love me, do you?'

She returned my hand to her waist. 'And I'm not clever enough for you. They kept me in Standard 4 till I left. But there's one thing I'll do,' she said, sitting up briskly and speaking like a teacher beginning a lesson. 'I'll learn you how to kiss properly.'

Learn me she did, dear Daisy, and I'll always be grateful.

All the while I was thinking these things out, or at

least getting them a bit clearer, I was walking. The road led downriver parallel to our own Western Road. On my right was the Tyne, bleak and cold in winter, warm and odorous in summer, but always silent and invisible except where rough ground separated one shipyard or factory from another. Then I could see the lights of my town on the other side and hear, and even fancy I recognised, voices made thin and ethereal by the wide night air and the immense starry sky.

To my left, streets ran uphill where Northumberland children skipped and played, ran to the corner-end pubs for supper beer in huge milk jugs on summer evenings, and in winter sledged down the glinting pavements on boards and boxes, shooting out into the main road, mercifully traffic-less at this late hour.

Here and there I passed a church or chapel, and, if it was Friday and choir-practice night, drew near to the Victorian-Gothic lighted windows, and stood amongst hot and dusty or cold and rime-covered privet and laurel—according to the season, to hear the singing. I have always found the power and passion of Wesleyan singing deeply moving. 'O thou who camest from above,' sung to 'Hereford', that subtle and heart-piercing tune, could and can move me to tears. So could poor mad Cowper's hymns, and even those which had no poetry or genuine devotion were lifted by the sincerity of the singers to an emotional height they did not deserve.

But did God exist? I asked myself sadly as I walked on down the road. If he did, and if he was love, why were there barefoot bairns crying on pub steps, and tramps stretched out in shop doorways padding themselves out with filthy newspapers? And why were frail girls of fifteen and raddled hags of fifty cutting across the very road I was walking along to disappear down paths that led to the darkness of foreign boats lying against the quayside. In imagination I followed them to the lowered gangway, the obscene bargaining in pidgin English, the squalid acts in cramped cabins and smelly fo'c'sles, the furtive exchange of money, and the weary trail back to a Wallsend slum street. Poverty and wickedness (as I thought it), how could they exist if God did and was omnipotent?

Now and again old men begged from me to make up the fourpence they needed to get a bed at one of the many doss-houses (this was when I was older, of course) and now and again a girl would turn and keep in step for a few paces and smile sideways and wait for me to accept her mute offering of herself. I was never able to. Pity for the poverty that was so often the cause of this sordid way of supplementing a poor wage or helping to support a sick or unemployed father was always stronger than lust. I was, too, always a romantic, and could never desire without love.

One girl I often met, pale and rather beautiful, but marked already with T.B., that scourge of our youth, wore a black fur coat and always smiled at me without any invitation at all. I liked to think we passed as the ships did, each, as the naval manuals have it, 'on our lawful occasions' and that the silent greeting was innocent and disinterested, due only to a passive sympathy between two young people half attracted to one another without knowing why.

Nothing much ever really happened to me on these night walks in the next county, but boy and young man, I had to escape every now and then and this was my only means. By the time I had walked a couple of miles down river and was at the lower ferry I was tired and ready for home. Behind me the streets, emptying of children, were filling with workmen coming off late shifts, and with the pubs spilling out their drunks like herring from a trawler. There was noisy singing, Irish mostly, except for the inevitable 'Blaydon Races', and sometimes fighting.

The second 'nighted ferry', named after the director of the shipbuilding firm I worked for, crossed slowly against a keen wind that swept up from the three-mile-away sea. I had never seen the man, and later, when we were all on the dole and hungry through the bankruptcy of his firm, found myself hating this rich pompous industrialist (as we all thought him). It was many years later, on a visit to the town I had long since left, that I noticed a brass plate in the parish church where I had often paid more attention to the new hat gracing Ethel's head than the service, and learned that he had lost his son at Gallipoli, and was, whatever his professional faults, a man born to suffering and loss like the rest of us.

But that was years away yet. The slump was only beginning, and our yard was still building gaunt red-leaded tankers. I could see the *British Freedom* looming up a stone's throw from the ferry, and the *Duchess of York*, the last ship we ever built for the Royal Navy. She went down at Crete sometime in the Second World War which none of us thought possible in those days of anti-war books and disarmament. Once we touched our own side of the river, there was only the walk home through familiar streets. Naturally I mix the various occasions because I suppose I made this night walk several times a year from when I was about fourteen until I was twenty-one and (technically, at any rate) a man.

The last tram would be coming in from Shields with its quota of out-of-town drinkers and lads who had been after the girls along King Street and Ocean Road. Everyone fanned out towards the suburbs, and I sometimes had company—a confidential drunk who complained about his wife, or a former schoolmate boasting about the girl he might have (but probably hadn't) seduced on the dry sand under the pier. But generally I was on my own and preferred to be. I felt like a traveller returning from a foreign country. Empty Grenville Street, dark except for its forlorn lamps, and a light here and there in a bedroom window, was after all dear and home. If I hadn't solved my problems I had at least wrestled with them, and could relax, and drink my soothing cocoa, and go thankfully to bed.

There was my book—Housman's intoxicating poems, or Ruskin's prose, or Mary Webb's doom-laden Shropshire novels—there my precious scrap of red candle and 'the cool kindliness of sheets'. Perhaps I only thought I had been thinking, but I felt there was some virtue in trying. Soon I put the book down, blew out my light, and in the acrid dark, except where our lamp threw golden bars of Venetian blind on the flaking wall, turned over and began to say my hasty prayers.